AN ARTS FOUNDATION COURSE

UNIT 16 THE GREAT EXHIBITION AND RE-READING 'HARD TIMES'

Prepared by John Golby for the Course Team

UNIT 17 INTERDISCIPLINARY STUDY: AN INTRODUCTION

Prepared by Stuart Brown, Nicola Durbridge, Arthur Marwick, Richard Middleton, Gill Perry, Gerrylynn Roberts and Michael Rossington for the Course Team

The Open University

Cover: The interior of the Great Crystal Palace — the transept looking north (*Illustrated London News*, 7 June 1851, pp. 526—7)

The Open University
Walton Hall
Milton Keynes
MK7 6AA

First published 1986; second edition 1991

Copyright © 1986 and 1991 The Open University

All rights reserved. No part of this publication may be reproduced, stored in a retrieval system or transmitted in any form or by any means, without written permission from the publisher or a licence from the Copyright Licensing Agency Limited. Details of such licences (for reprographic reproduction) may be obtained from the Copyright Licensing Agency Ltd., 33—34 Alfred Place, London WC1E 7DP.

Designed by the Graphic Design Group of the Open University.

Typeset by Medcalf Type Ltd, Bicester, Oxon
Printed in the United Kingdom by
Courier International Ltd., Tiptree, Essex.

ISBN 0 7492 1033 8

This unit forms part of an Open University course; a complete list of the units is on the back cover.

If you have not enrolled on the course and would like to buy this or other Open University material, please write to Open University Educational Enterprises, 12 Cofferidge Close, Stony Stratford, Milton Keynes, MK11 1BY, United Kingdom. If you wish to enquire about enrolling as an Open University student, please write to The Open University, PO Box 625, Walton Hall, Milton Keynes, MK1 1TY, United Kingdom.

2.1

PREFACE

You have now completed the first part of the course. Your study of the five disciplines — history, literature, music and art history — has introduced the various methodological approaches used within these disciplines and, for the rest of the course, you will be applying these approaches in a large interdisciplinary study of Britain in the period 1850–90. Unit 16 marks the start of the interdisciplinary study. It introduces you to Britain in the 1850s with a major event, the Great Exhibition of 1851.

There are two main reasons why we have decided to start with an examination of the Great Exhibition. First, the Great Exhibition was an occasion which brought together in the Crystal Palace in Hyde Park a vast array of exhibits of machinery, manufacturers and fine arts from all over the world. As well as providing an opportunity to demonstrate that Britain was the leading industrial nation in the world, the Exhibition was a popular event and 6 million visitors attended it during the five months that it was open to the public. Second, the Great Exhibition appears to provide, at least at first glance, a quite different picture of Britain in the 1850s, from the one depicted by Charles Dickens in *Hard Times*. The Great Exhibition was intended as a symbol of harmony and confidence in the industrial development of Britain. In the words of its organizers, it was designed, 'to present a true test and living picture of the point of development at which the whole of mankind has arrived . . . and a new starting point, from which all nations will be able to direct their further exertions.' But while the organizers of the Exhibition were optimistic, some other people were highly critical of some of the changes that were taking place within industrial Britain. The attitude of Charles Dickens towards many of these changes was often ambivalent, but in *Hard Times*, although it is only one aspect of the novel, he shows a concern for British industrial society where, in his opinion, conflict is more prevalent than harmony. However, rather than providing contradictory pictures of British society, we hope that by examining the Great Exhibition and *Hard Times* in some detail, you will discover that they complement rather than contradict each other and that they both shed valuable light on a society which was undergoing rapid social, economic and political changes.

You should spend half of one week's study on 'The Great Exhibition' and the other half on re-reading *Hard Times*. *Hard Times* will be touched upon in all the later units and considered in detail in Units 22–26; it is essential that you spend time re-reading the book so that the events and issues discussed in the novel are clear in your mind.

Unit 17 *Interdisciplinary Study: An Introduction* consolidates information about the period which you will have gathered from Unit 16 and Units 1–3 *Introduction to History* and also discusses how the concepts and methods to which you have been introduced in the first half of the course are to be applied. You should spend a week on Unit 17 but it will probably be of help to you if you keep Unit 17 handy and refer to it from time to time when the themes are taken up and discussed in greater detail later on in the course.

Television programmes 16 and 17 are devoted to the Great Exhibition. The first programme *The Great Exhibition I: An Exercise in Industry* is primarily concerned with the construction of the Crystal Palace and the mechanical exhibits housed there. Television programme 17 *The Great Exhibition II: A Lesson in Taste?* examines Victorian notions of good design — 'taste' — by looking at some of the exhibits and the range of comments on them in the contemporary press.

Unit 16

THE GREAT EXHIBITION AND RE-READING 'HARD TIMES'

SET READING

As you work through Unit 16 you will need to refer to

John Golby (ed.) (1986) *Culture and Society in Britain 1850–1890* (Course Reader)

Charles Dickens (1989) *Hard Times* (Set Book)

BROADCASTING

Television programme 16 *The Great Exhibition I: An Exercise in Industry*

Television programme 17 *The Great Exhibition II: A Lesson in Taste?*

Radio programme 8 *Interview with Lord Briggs on Victorian Culture and Society*

PART I   THE GREAT EXHIBITION

OBJECTIVES

1   By the end of this part of the unit you should be able to understand why the Great Exhibition was presented in Britain in 1851 and what the aims of the organizers of the Exhibition were.

2   You should also be aware of how the Exhibition was for many people a symbol of progress and in this respect highlighted many of the dominant characteristics of the period including a belief in technology; a general feeling of confidence, particularly in respect to economic individualism and political liberalism; prosperity and comparative social harmony and a high seriousness and moral earnestness.

3   At the same time you should appreciate that despite this confidence a large section of the population was still living in a state of poverty and that there was a questioning of the concept of progress and a preoccupation not only with the future but with the mediaeval and the gothic.

1 THE OPENING OF THE EXHIBITION

At 11.30 am on the morning of Thursday 1 May 1851 Queen Victoria and her entourage left Buckingham Palace in nine state coaches to open 'The Great Exhibition of the Works of Industry of all Nations'. By the time she reached the site of the Exhibition at Hyde Park one quarter to half a million people were massed in the Royal Park. Inside the Crystal Palace, the enormous glass and iron building built especially for the occasion, 30,000 more privileged people were assembled. The opening ceremony was an imposing affair: massed choirs sang the National Anthem, the Archbishop of Canterbury offered up prayers and the ceremony was completed by the singing of Handel's *Hallelujah Chorus*.

With over 13,000 exhibitors from forty different countries and well over 100,000 items on display the Great Exhibition was the largest international exhibition ever assembled. The Exhibition Hall, the Crystal Palace, covered an area of 18 acres and not only was it the first structure in which cast iron and glass were used on such a large scale, but it was also the first building of its size to be constructed chiefly of prefabricated units. Wherever possible, building parts were standardized and as a result of this method of construction, together with a well-organized workforce which worked night and day, the building of the Crystal Palace was completed in the short space of twenty-two weeks. Considering that the land in Hyde Park was not handed over to the contractors until 30 July 1850, it was a remarkable achievement; not only was the building itself completed but virtually all the exhibits were ready on display for the opening only nine months later.

One half of the exhibition space was devoted to Great Britain and her colonies and the remaining half to the rest of the world. The Exhibition was also divided into ~~four~~ six sections: raw materials; machinery; manufactures*, and fine arts. Despite these categories the Exhibition assembled under one roof a bewilderingly wide range of goods and designs. There was a mixture of ornately decorated articles including inkstands that looked like thistles, a 'Sportsman's knife' with more than 80 blades, together with such exclusively utilitarian inventions as gas cooking stoves and washing and mangling machines. On the one hand, there were on display many examples of modern machinery with interchangeable parts which heralded mass production

[handwritten margin note: 2 TYPES OF MANUFACTURE 1) TEXTILE FABRICS 2) METALLIC, VITREOUS & CERAMIC SIX CLASSES ÷ INTO 30 SUB-SECTION]

Figure 1 Letterhead illuminating the Crystal Palace, London, 1851. (Photo: Allwood, John (1977) The Great Exhibitiion, Studio Vista)

techniques, and, on the other, there were numerous exhibits demonstrating traditional craftsmanship which had been carried on for centuries. French porcelain was displayed by the side of recent inventions, and items demonstrating tremendous technical and material advances were housed under the same roof as Pugin's 'Mediaeval Court'. Perhaps the only unifying factor in the whole exhibition was an obvious confidence in the introduction and application of the new industrial processes as well as pride in the skill of the more traditional craftsmen.

The organization of the Exhibition was under the control of a group of Royal Commissioners of whom the two most hard-working and committed members were Albert, the Prince Consort, and a civil servant, Henry Cole (1802–82). Both were members of the Society of Arts (in fact, Prince Albert was President of the Society), which had promoted three industrial design exhibitions in 1847, 1848 and 1849. All three of these exhibitions were, however, confined to home produced exhibits. The much more ambitions idea of a large-scale international exhibition was one which they pursued tirelessly throughout 1850 and 1851.

 Exercise

From the start, as you'll see from some letters and a diary extract describing the opening day, the Exhibition was regarded as a great success. But is this the whole story? Read extracts 1.2 from Lord Macaulay's Diary, 1.3 a letter from the Duchess of Gloucester and 1.4 a letter from Queen Victoria in *Culture and Society in Britain 1850–1890* (Course Reader).

1 What particularly pleased the writers about the day?

2 What did these writers fear might happen to spoil the day?

 Answers and discussion

1 All of the writers emphasized the impressive nature of the spectacle and both Macaulay and the Duchess of Gloucester mentioned the good humour and behaviour of the crowd. While Queen Victoria reserved most of her praise and delight for her 'beloved Albert' who had worked so hard to achieve this successful day, the Duchess of Gloucester made a particular point of stating how beneficial it was that the foreigners should witness the affection of the people towards the Queen and her family.

There is little doubt that this last remark, contained a certain element of smugness. Britain's royal family was deeply entrenched as an institution and much more popular than continental monarchs. But this popularity was comparatively new.

Victoria's two predecessors, George IV and William IV, with their many mistresses and illegitimate children, had died unmourned by the country at large and in 1837, when she came to the throne, the prestige of the crown was at a very low ebb. Since her marriage to Albert of Saxe-Coburg-Gotha in 1840, Victoria and her husband had worked hard to improve the position of the monarchy. One way in which they had endeared themselves, at least to the respectable middle classes, was by presenting a life style which contrasted sharply with that of George and William. Albert and Victoria set an example of respectable and harmonious family life with Victoria seeming an 'ideal' wife and mother. The seventh of Victoria's nine children had been born in 1850.

2 Macaulay mentioned the possibility of a demonstration of some sort on the part of 'the Socialists' and, although he believed Madame de Lieven's fears to be unfounded he did repeat her warning of 'a horrible explosion'. The Duchess of Gloucester made a vague reference to the 'anxiety and trouble' that Albert had undergone during the setting up of the Exhibition and Victoria mentioned the strong opposition to the Exhibition from a 'set of fashionables and Protectionists'.

Perhaps it is not surprising that many respectable Londoners were concerned at the thought of so many people from Europe and other parts of Britain descending on the capital for the Exhibition. Remember, nothing on the scale of this event had ever before been held in London. A variety of fears was expressed from a number of quarters. There were Protectionists who were opposed to the idea of allowing foreign countries to exhibit their goods in London; there were Protestants who predicted that London would be swamped by Roman Catholics from the continent, and there were those who were convinced that the Exhibition would attract 'the criminal classes' and that instances of robbery and violence would increase sharply. In the House of Commons, the MP for Lincoln, Colonel Sibthorp, accused the organizers of the Exhibition of introducing 'among us foreign stuff of every description . . . All the bad characters at present scattered over the country will be attracted to Hyde Park. This being the case I would advise persons residing near the Park to keep a sharp look out for their silver forks and spoons and servant maids.'

It would be wrong, however, merely to poke fun at these fears. After all, it was only three years earlier, in 1848, that a wave of attempted revolutions swept through most parts of Europe, and although no revolution was attempted in Britain, a monster Chartist demonstration which demanded, among other things, universal manhood suffrage, had taken place in London on 10 April 1848. This threat to public order was taken very seriously by the government and the Duke of Wellington, who had been put in charge of London's defences, ensured that the city was garrisoned by thousands of policemen, 8,000 soldiers and over 150,000 special constables. This event and the revolutions on the continent were still vivid in many people's minds. Understandably they dreaded the thought of fresh political riots and mob violence and so Madame de Lieven was not alone in believing that the Exhibition was 'a rash experiment'. But times were changing rapidly. A general rise in the standard of living and a reduction in taxes on food were two of the reasons why 'the men of action with whom the Socialists were threatening us' did not turn up. Nevertheless, the fear of working-class discontent had not entirely disappeared and although on this occasion the Duke of Wellington did not mobilize any of the armed forces, the City and Metropolitan police force was augmented by 900 men.

2 THE THEMES OF THE EXHIBITION

In 1850 Prince Albert made a speech at the Mansion House to dignitaries from both Britain and abroad. In it he spoke of 'the peculiar character and claims' of the period which convinced him that the time was exactly right for putting on an exhibition of the works of all nations.

 Exercise

Read extract I.1 in the Course Reader, taken from this speech.

1   What were the reasons given by Prince Albert for the early 1850s being particularly suited for such an exhibition?

2   What do you think Prince Albert means by 'progress'?

 Answers and discussion

1   (a) That for the first time in history the world was on the point of 'the realization of the unity of mankind'. This was attainable because of the blessings of the Almighty but could be achieved completely only if there was a policy of peace and love not only between individuals but between nations.
(b) A major reason for these advances was the application of science to understanding 'the laws by which the Almighty governs His creation'.
(c) One aspect of this was the 'great principle of division of labour' which 'is being extended to all branches of science, industry and art'.

2   Progress was dependent on the application of science and, by applying science to industry, advances would continue to be made as long as they were 'intrusted to the stimulus of competition and capital'. Peace too was needed for progress to be maintained. Not just peace between nations but also within nations. An essential prerequisite for advance was an industrious and a politically and socially quiescent workforce.

So, the purpose of the Exhibition was, in Albert's words, to give 'a true test and a living picture of the point of development at which the whole of mankind has arrived, and a new starting point, from which all nations will be able to direct their further exertions'. Progress, religion, science, free competition, capitalism, work and peace were all factors which had contributed, so Prince Albert believed, towards the enormous industrial advances which had taken place during the nineteenth century. Indeed, the last two — the gospels of work and peace — were the two great themes of the Exhibition of 1851. The aim was to honour 'the working bees of the world's hive' and to demonstrate that 'the workers of all types stand forth as the really good men'. Of course, the gospel of work was nothing new. Thomas Carlyle (1795–1881) and many others had for years preached the importance of work and mottoes like 'An endless significance lies in Work' and 'Not what I have, but what I do is my kingdom' were commonplace in Victorian homes and workplaces. But Albert was not so much concerned with the old traditional work patterns. He was convinced that great advances in civilization would occur through the application of science to industry and the introduction of mechanical processes into manufactures. One outcome of this would be the division of labour in industry. But some other contemporaries were not so sanguine about mechanization and the organization of labour along these lines. They argued that although goods might be produced in greater quantities and at lower prices, the division of labour reduced skills and job satisfaction and, indeed, labour became degraded and dehumanized. This viewpoint was portrayed in the description by Charles Dickens of the factory textile town of Coketown in *Hard Times*. So, although the Exhibition had on show the skills of traditional craftsmen as well as examples of new industrial machinery, the controversy about work and mechanization was one which was hotly maintained throughout this period.

The second great theme of the Exhibition was peace. Not only was peace regarded as a virtue, because it conformed to Christian teaching, but many manufacturers and industrialists believed it to be an essential condition if new international markets were to be developed and extended. In this last respect the idea of peace went hand in hand with one of the major economic principles prevalent in Britain, namely free trade. If, so it was argued, all countries did away with tariff barriers and entered into open competition a much needed stability would be brought to international trade. Economic ties of self-interest would encourage international interdependence, and this in turn would inevitably bring world peace. It was hoped that the Exhibition would play its part in persuading the leaders of foreign powers to move their countries towards free trade but, understandably, the fear of being swamped by British manufactured goods made foreigners reluctant to adopt free trade policies.

Although the principle of free trade was to remain firmly entrenched in Britain, the desire to maintain world peace was not so firmly held and within three years of the opening of the Exhibition, Britain, along with France, was at war with Russia in the Crimea.

Not only was the hope for permanent peace disturbed by the outbreak of the Crimean War but religion itself, although it appeared prominently in Albert's speech, was certainly not as central to the lives of the people of Britain, especially those of the urban working classes, as he may have hoped and certainly it was not as unifying a force as he believed. Protestant Britain was still suspicious of Catholic Europe and one of the major political problems with which the British government was struggling in 1850 and 1851 was what its reaction should be to a papal pronouncement that Roman Catholic dioceses should be reintroduced into Britain and a regular Roman Catholic hierarchy be restored. Certainly, this announcement by the Pope had brought a strong and noisy reaction from protestants and dissenters throughout the country. But although many sections of the population were seemingly deeply worried about a Roman Catholic revival in Britain, by no means a majority of the country's inhabitants appeared to be active churchgoers. A census taken on Sunday 30 March 1851 in England and Wales, which was published in early 1854, showed that out of a total population of some 18 millions, only about 7¼ million attended some sort of church service on that day. Perhaps what was equally alarming to many Victorians was that although the Church of England was the established Church, only about 20 per cent of the population had attended Anglican services.

One reason, not mentioned by Prince Albert, for holding the Great Exhibition, was to show to the rest of the world that Britain was not only the most prosperous nation but also the industrial centre of the world. As we have seen, Britain and her colonies received half of the floor space at the Exhibition; the other half was left for the rest of the world.

By 1851 Britain was well-known as the workshop of the world. Note, however, the use of the word 'workshop' and not factory. For, apart from cotton textiles, British industries in mid-century were still composed of comparatively small units of production. Britain was not only the world's workshop, she was, in the words of Professor Briggs, 'the world's shipbuilder, the world's carrier, the world's banker, and the world's clearing-house'. No wonder free trade was popular in Britain when the country was in such a strong position to influence world markets.

Above all, the Exhibition reflected the strong degree of confidence that existed in the country as a result of the growth in industrial wealth. It was a confidence based on the firm belief that prosperity had been brought about as a result of free enterprise, free trade and individual endeavour. Maxims such as 'Heaven helps those who help themselves' were prevalent in 1851. To many

12

there appeared no limit to what could be achieved by free enterprise and self-help. The Exhibition itself seemed a good example of this. It had been financed entirely by private capital and received no government aid at all, and the designer of the Crystal Palace, Joseph Paxton (1801–65), who had developed the idea from a glass Lily House which he had built when a gardener at Chatsworth, appeared the epitome of the ideal of self-help. One of the most popular writers of the period, Samuel Smiles (1812–1904) refers to Paxton in his book *Self-Help* which first appeared in 1859. In this book, of which 55,000 copies were sold in its first five years of publication, Smiles cites numerous examples of men who although starting from humble beginnings had, by their own efforts, achieved greatness. Paxton had started life as the seventh son of a relatively poor Bedfordshire farmer and Smiles praised him as a man of 'diligent self-improvement' whose life had been one of hard work and 'assiduous cultivation of knowledge'. Undoubtedly Paxton was a man of great talent and energy. Nevertheless there is another side to the story and when Smiles described Paxton as a man 'who cultivates opportunities' he perhaps was not thinking of such self-seeking activities as making a financially advantageous marriage, obtaining the patronage of the Duke of Devonshire and making a fortune on the Stock Exchange by investing in railway shares during the boom in the 1840s.

Again when Henry Cole made a speech extolling the virtues of the Exhibition and claiming that it had been built 'independent of taxes and the employment of slaves' some critics of the Exhibition attacked him by declaring that it all depended on what he meant by 'slaves'. They maintained that certain sections of the population were, despite the supposed material advances, still living in poverty. *Punch* magazine published a cartoon pointing out to Prince Albert what would be a more typical Exhibition, namely, exhibits from the depressed sections of the working class – a woman dressmaker, an aged casual labourer, a shoemaker and a tailor's assistant. *Punch* had deliberately chosen four trades which were notoriously badly paid; but note that the textile power loom factory worker, the trade of Stephen Blackpool in *Hard Times*, is not included here.

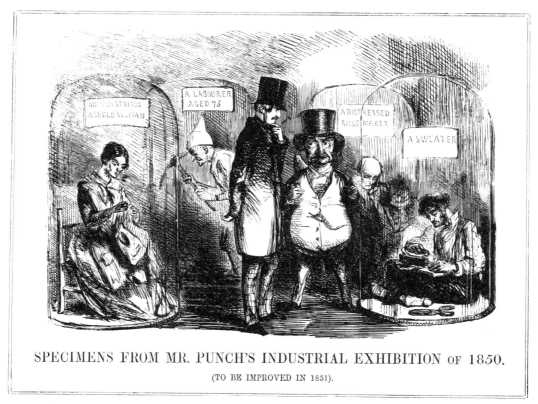

SPECIMENS FROM MR. PUNCH'S INDUSTRIAL EXHIBITION OF 1850.

(TO BE IMPROVED IN 1851).

*Figure 2 'Specimens from Mr Punch's Industrial Exhibition of 1850', cartoon.
(Photo:* Punch, *Vol. 18, January–June 1850)*

Despite Dickens's depiction of the grim life led by factory workers in the Lancashire textile towns, conditions, relative to those trades mentioned by *Punch*, were not bad. Certainly much of the work was monotonous and carried out in poor conditions but, for example, power loom workers like Stephen Blackpool were much better paid than the hand-loom weavers who worked from their own homes but who were unable to produce goods as cheaply or in the quantities of factory-made articles. Also, unlike most other workers throughout the country, working conditions and hours for cotton textile workers were protected by government legislation. Indeed, in 1850 they were among the very first group of workers in the country to win a statutory Saturday half-day holiday. But the work patterns and routine of factory workers were comparatively new and strange in a country where far more people worked on the land than in any single industry, so that as W.L. Burn has pointed out, an agricultural labourer in Dorset would have found the diet of a skilled worker in a Lancashire factory 'sumptuous beyond his wildest dreams but he would have been astonished at the punctuality required of him in the mills'.

Nevertheless, despite the growing prosperity in the country, a large section of the population lived in conditions of severe poverty. The condition of the poor was a national problem and it remained so throughout the century. It was not until the end of the century in the 1880s and 1890s that reliable attempts were made to measure the extent of poverty in some urban areas and then it was established that something like 30 per cent of the population were living in a state of poverty.

Overall, though, there was a great albeit an uneven growth in prosperity. There was more money about and more things to spend it on than ever before. The many ornate town halls, industrial buildings and churches and chapels, together with the domestic buildings built around this time, bear witness to this wealth. But perhaps the most obvious sign of the increasing prosperity of the middle and upper classes can be seen in the enormous increase in numbers of domestic servants during the century. In 1801 there were 600,000; by 1851 the number was over 1,300,000 and constituted over 13 per cent of the entire labour force in the country. By 1881 servants numbered 3,000,000 or nearly 16 per cent of the labour force. The vast majority of servants were women and it has been estimated that of girls between the ages of fifteen and twenty, one in three was a domestic servant. Some sections of the working classes, especially the skilled workers, also had some share in this prosperity and during the period 1850 to 1875 their real wages increased by around one-third.

It was partly because of the general improvement in the economy that working class discontent, so noticeable in the 1830s and 1840s, had become much more muted by the early 1850s. But that is not to say that the working classes were completely inactive (note the cotton strike at Preston in 1854 which so influenced Charles Dickens in his writing of *Hard Times*). A number of important unions were formed in the 1850s. For example, in 1851 the Amalgamated Society of Engineers, the forerunner of the AUEW, was founded.

 Exercise

Look closely at Figure 3, a membership certificate for the Amalgamated Society of Engineers.

1   What are the sentiments expressed in this design?

2   Do these sentiments harmonize or clash with the sentiments expressed by Prince Albert in his speech made in 1850?

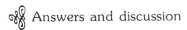 Answers and discussion

1   The dove and angel at the top of the picture obviously symbolize peace. One workman is refusing to mend the God of War's sword, whereas the workman on the right is accepting a scroll from the Goddess of Peace.

Figure 3   Certificate of the Amalgamated Sopciety of Engineers, Machinists, Millwrights, Smiths, and Pattern Makers, 1851. (Reproduced by courtesy of the Amalgamated Union of Engineering Workers)

Associated with war is disunity (the figure breaking one stick) and with peace goes unity (the figure failing to break a bundle of sticks).

There is no doubt that the Union approves of the technological advances made over the previous half century because three great inventors, Crompton, Arkwright and Watt (in a toga) are given prominence. In addition, pride in progress is depicted by the railway train in the bottom left of the picture bringing raw materials to the 'factory' where they are converted with the help of new technology (the steam engine in the centre) into finished products, which are then exported overseas by steamships. The horn of plenty symbolizes the prosperity that will come with peace, unity and industry.

2   These sentiments fit in very closely with Albert's beliefs. After all, the two great themes of the Exhibition were work and peace. These workers, too, believed in the progress that Albert stressed in his speech in 1850. The only point of difference was the idea of unity. Albert did talk of 'ready assistance' between individuals but, on this membership certificate, unity refers to the members of the ASE. Only by unity would the Union survive. On the other hand it is important to note that this was a union of skilled men with a membership of only around 33,000 and its declared object was to do nothing 'illegally or indiscreetly, but on all occasions to perform the greatest amount of

benefit for ourselves without injury to others'. They were much more concerned about the status of their individual trades than with the overall place of working men within society.

Compared with the discontent and disquiet within the country in the years following the ending of the Napoleonic Wars and during the early 1830s and 1840s, the working classes were much more quiescent by the early 1850s. Still, although unions like the ASE did not pursue radical policies or directly challenge the economic system, they were insistent on developing specific rights as trade unions. One successful outcome of this policy was that it made it easier in the 1870s and 1880s for unskilled workers to organize themselves into unions.

3 REACTIONS TO THE EXHIBITION

I have in the previous section already touched on a number of reactions to the Exhibition. Certainly within all sections of the community, from the Monarchy to the working class, the confident belief in progress, of which the Exhibition was a manifestation, was deeply held. The Exhibition had a direct and positive effect on some of its visitors. For example, William Whiteley (1831–1907), later to make a fortune as a manufacturer and retailer of glass products, was so impressed by the Crystal Palace itself that he determined that at some time in the future he would equip retail stores with large glass windows. But, as we have seen, not all reactions were favourable. Opposition ranged from extremist crank views to those who believed that the money spent on the Exhibition would have been better used in improving the lot of the poor, through critics like Charles Dickens whose attitude towards technological progress was ambivalent and who 'had an instinctive feeling against the Exhibition of a faint, inexplicable sort', to some artists who were highly critical of the Exhibition. William Morris (1834–96) thought the Exhibition 'wonderfully ugly' and Edward Burne-Jones (1833–98) regarded it as 'cheerless' and 'monotonous'. Pugin (1812–52), whose Mediaeval Court on display at the Exhibition looked not forward to a scientific age but back towards the fourteenth century, called the Crystal Palace a 'glass monster'. Nevertheless, many influential people believed that this 'glass monster' should be preserved and in 1854 the Crystal Palace was moved from Hyde Park to a permanent site in Sydenham. (The Crystal Palace remained there until it was destroyed by fire in 1937.) In the same year, 1854, John Ruskin (1819–1900), the leading art critic in the country, wrote a short article in which he expressed his views about the Crystal Palace.

Exercise

Read extract IV. 5 'John Ruskin, "*The Opening of the Crystal Palace*" ' in the Course Reader and then answer the following questions:

1   Does Ruskin have anything good to say about the Crystal Palace?

2   In what ways is he critical of the Crystal Palace?

3   What does Ruskin regard as 'the evil which is being wrought by this age'?

Answers

1   Yes. He acknowledges the 'mechanical ingenuity' which went into its construction and he sees its value as a national museum. He believes that it will provide opportunities of intellectual stimulation for working men and women which is preferable to 'hours once wasted'. One of the questions you should consider is whether visitors to the Great Exhibition held mechanical ingenuity and novelty in higher esteem than the practical inventions which were on display. You will find discussion of this question in television programme 16 *The Great Exhibition I: An Exercise in Industry*.

2   His main criticisms are directed not towards the Crystal Palace itself but to what he regards as the excessively lavish praise it has received from all quarters including 'nearly all the professors of art of our time'. Despite its virtues Ruskin stresses that 'mechanical ingenuity is *not* the essence either of painting or architecture: and largeness of dimension does not necessarily involve nobleness of design'. What worries Ruskin is that there is too much interest in mechanical ingenuity while truly great works of art, such as those of J. M. W. Turner in Britain and the Venetian masters in Italy, were not only being neglected but ignored.

3   Here Ruskin wanders away from discussing the Crystal Palace and argues that partly because there is such an interest in technological advances (of which the Crystal Palace is a fine example) there is a growing movement to restore old buildings and sculptures. But he is convinced that despite all modern techniques 'architecture and painting (can only) be restored when the dead can be raised'.

Ruskin saw technological advances and the division of labour not as providing progress but rather as a movement towards degrading the value of work and denying individuality. As a result he feared for art itself. He particularly detested the numerous exhibits which were made of 'imitation' materials — papier-mâché to simulate wood, imitation marble and so on, and he saw only grotesqueness in the unnecessary ornateness of some of the designs. The ability to use new industrial processes not only to produce goods but to produce 'the artwork' on them, and the advantage of producing goods more cheaply if imitation materials were used, were not reasons which Ruskin could accept. To Ruskin 'whatever the material you chose to work with, your art is base if it does not bring out the distinctive qualities of that material'.

The other side of the argument was put forward lucidly by Dr Whewell (1794–1866), a mathematician, historian and philosopher of science, and Master of Trinity College, Cambridge, who in a talk about the Great Exhibition given in November 1851 admitted that some of the arts and goods from the less advanced countries possessed 'a degree of splendour and artistical richness, which is not found among ourselves'. However, he went on to argue that whereas in those countries the arts were 'mainly exercised to gratify the tastes of the few', Britain supplies 'the wants of the many . . . the machine with its million fingers works for millions of purchasers, while in remote countries, where magnificence and savagery stand side by side, tens of thousands work for one'. That is, he claimed, the area in which Britain's superiority lay. Whewell was fully aware that what was important about the Exhibition was not so much the fine art exhibits or the artwork on manufactured goods but rather the new machinery and the products that could be produced by these machines. In this respect Whewell reflected the attitude of the Exhibition Committee which during the Exhibition distributed 164 Council Medals among the 13,000 exhibitors. Of the 78 medals that were awarded to UK exhibitors, 52 went to machinery, 18 to manufacturers, 6 to raw materials and only 2 to fine arts. Some of the reasons for this are discussed in television programme 17 *The Great Exhibition II: A Lesson in Taste?*

4 WHO VISITED THE EXHIBITION?

When the Great Exhibition was opened the price of admission was five shillings (25p). This, of course, excluded all but the better off. But after the first few weeks admission prices were reduced to two shillings and sixpence (12½p) on Friday and one shilling (5p) from Monday to Thursday. Only Saturday remained a five shilling day. Joseph Paxton had suggested that entry to the Exhibition should be free but this idea had been rejected by the Committee on the grounds that all the petty criminals and rowdy elements in London would invade the Exhibition. But the real reason for their refusal was the need to obtain revenue to cover the costs of the Exhibition. This was a more compelling reason than the fear of noisy mobs. Nevertheless, with the onset of the 'shilling day' a different sort of visitor arrived at the Exhibition. Of the 6 million visitors who attended the Exhibition in the five months and eleven days that it was open, 4½ million, or approximately three-quarters of the total attenders, came on shilling days. (The population of Great Britain in 1851 was nearly 21 million of which about 2½ million lived in London.) Attendances might well have been higher still if the Exhibition had been open on Sundays but a growing Sabbatarian movement and a deputation of leading Evangelicals to the Prime Minister ensured that permission would not be granted for Sunday opening.

 Exercise

Read extract 1.5 in the Course Reader and then answer the following questions.

1 Why does the writer think 1851 is an opportune time to hold the Exhibition?

2 What does the writer see as the advantages of the Exhibition?

3 What does the writer mean by the 'rational purposes' of the Exhibition?

 Answers and discussion

1 Travel to and from the Exhibition would have been particularly difficult if it had been held only a few years earlier because the railway system would not have been able to cope with the numbers, either from abroad or within Britain, who wished to attend the Exhibition. Within a period of twenty years a virtually countrywide railway network of some 7,000 miles had been laid and about a third of this had been built in the period 1846–50. By the time of the Great Exhibition the major railway trunk lines in the country had been laid.

The rapid development of railways had transformed the face of Britain. Not only had it revolutionized the travel habits of the people of Britain, it had also had an enormous effect on British industry. Goods could now be transported more quickly and much more cheaply. It would have been almost impossible to build the Crystal Palace in the time available if it had not been for the railways. For example, all the glass for the Palace (900,000 sq. ft. weighing 400 tons) was transported from a firm outside Birmingham to London by train much more quickly than if it had been moved by road or canal.

2 The writer believes that the Exhibition was contributing to the breaking down of animosities and prejudices especially of the French towards the British. Whether this was true or not, the Exhibition attracted a large number of people from abroad. Between April and September 1851, 58,427 foreigners entered Britain, compared with only 15,514 for the same period in the previous year. Of this 58,000, 27,000 came from France, 10,500 were Germans and 5,000 came from the USA. The other advantage claimed by the writer links up with question 3.

British Railway System 1845	British Railway System 1851

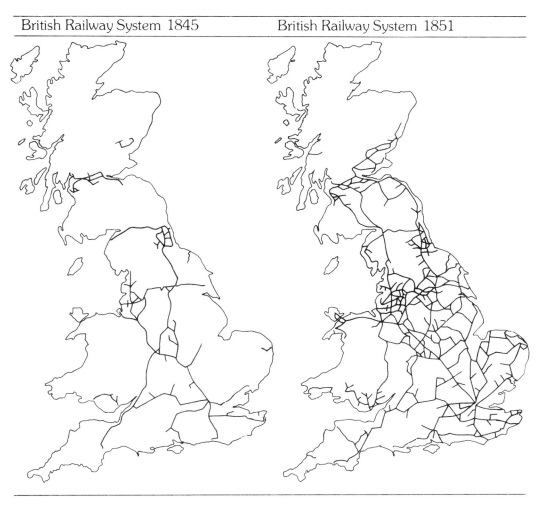

Figure 4   The growth of the railway network. On the left, the British railway system in 1845 and on the right in 1851.

3   The writer means by 'rational' an experience which is not only pleasurable but which at the same time is instructive. This, he maintains, is another advantage of the Exhibition: working people have the opportunity to visit a wonderful spectacle and are able to take away with them 'a remembrance of pleasure and instruction to last them for the remainder of their lives'.

You may remember, in his essay on the Crystal Palace, Ruskin wrote that it was better to be dedicated to useful pursuits rather than 'wasted hours'. The problem of how people should use their leisure was of great concern to many of the middle classes at this time. In particular, they took an active interest in how the working classes spent their leisure time. Indeed, they felt that the working classes could do much to improve their position and could live comparatively prosperously if only they spent less money on drinking and gambling and more time on 'improving' pastimes. If they could be weaned from 'worthless' activities to pastimes which were educational, then they would be in a better position to help themselves. It has been argued that by attempting to direct the working classes towards more rational recreation, what the governing classes were really attempting to create was an orderly, politically quiescent and hard-working workforce. But this is too simple an explanation. There is no doubt that the governing classes wanted to distract the poor from their misery and from radical politics but that does not mean they were devoid of philanthropic concerns. Henry Mayhew (1812–87), who was one of the foremost writers of the time exposing the plight of the labouring poor, saw rational recreations in general and the Great Exhibition in particular as a great opportunity for the working classes. He said of the Exhibition, 'it is intended to

19

form the highest kind of school in which the highest knowledge is designed to be conveyed in the best possible manner, in combination with the highest amusement'.

So the Exhibition was seen as a wonderful occasion for fusing recreation with instruction and thereby improving the lot and the minds of the working classes.

The railway system played an important role in making the Great Exhibition a success. Cheap railway excursion enabled working class people to travel from all parts of Britain to London. They travelled in such numbers that some railway companies were stretched almost to breaking point. Just one of the numerous railway companies existing in 1851, the London and North Western, carried some three-quarters of a million passengers to London in excursion trains alone during the period when the one shilling day was in force. Working mens' clubs, Mechanics' Institutes and a whole host of other organizations provided opportunities for working men to save up for their trip to the Great Exhibition.

One man who saw the enormous potential profit to be made from this was Thomas Cook. He not only organized saving clubs for working men but he negotiated with the Midland railway for reduced rail fares. The return trip from Leeds to London was five shillings whilst the Great Exhibition was on and during this period Cook was responsible for bringing 165,000, or roughly 3 per cent of the total attendance, to the Exhibition. Railway excursion trips were not new in 1851 but the Exhibition played an important part in making people aware for the first time of the potential of the railways as part of a leisure industry which was within the price range of most people.

Employers who saw the benefits of rational recreations played their part. Some allowed time off work and others paid towards the cost of the trip to London. One agricultural implement-maker in Suffolk hired two ships and fitted them out with sleeping accommodation and catering facilities so that his workmen could go by sea from Suffolk to the Exhibition. The boats docked at a wharf in Westminster. The clergy in Sussex and Surrey were also responsible for enabling some 800 agricultural labourers to attend the Exhibition, at a cost of two shillings and two pence (11p) for the round trip.

Attendances at the Exhibition exceeded the organizers' wildest hopes. On average about 65,000 people visited the Exhibition each day and on the day before it closed, Tuesday 14 October, 109,915 people entered the Crystal Palace. With such high figures the Commissioners made a profit out of the Exhibition of some £186,000. Attendance charges were the main reason for this profit but income did come from other sources. For example, just under £2,000 came from charges for lavatories and wash rooms. The public provision of these facilities was comparatively new and it gives a good indication of the growing concern for public health and welfare. Here is an extract from the Commissioners' report.

Waiting Rooms and Washing Rooms

The Waiting-rooms were situated near the Refreshment-courts, those in the Transept being most frequented; the price was made higher, in order to induce the public to go to those which were not so central. No difference was made in the mode of fitting them up, or in the attendance. The total amount expended in constructing and fitting up the Water-closets and Washing-places was about £1600.

The Urinals for gentlemen were not charged for; 54 of the latter were provided. It would have been convenient if more accommodation had been provided in the Ladies Waiting-rooms, especially in the Transept. The following was the number of *Waiting-rooms* provided for each locality:

	Gentlemen	Ladies	Total	Charge
Transept	6	24	30	1d.
Eastern Refreshment-court	6	11	17	½d.
Western Refreshment-court	10	12	22	½d.
	22	47	69	

The current expenditure (Superintendent, 6 male attendants, 10 female) was £671.17s.3d.; current receipts, £2441.15s.9d. Excess of receipts over expenditure, £1769.18s.6d.

Washing-places. Expenditure (Superintendent, 3 male attendants, female attendants, 532 1lb soap, towels, etc.) £281.4s.8d.; deduct value of towels, etc. £8.10s. Receipts, £443.17s.6d. Excess of receipts over expenditure, £171.2s.10d.

It would appear that the use of the Washing-places fell off as the weather got colder:

The largest receipt from the Waiting-rooms on any one day was on the 8th October, and amounted to £32.16s.3d., on which day 11,171 persons made use of the Waiting-rooms. The number of visitors on that day was 109,760.

On that day each of the 1d. waiting-rooms must have been used by 229 persons, and the ½d. by 169 persons, during the 8 hours the building was open to the public.

It will appear that 827,820 persons paid for the use of these conveniences during the time of the Exhibition, or 14 per cent of the visitors, in addition to an equal if not larger proportion of gentlemen who made use of the urinals, of which no account was kept.

No apology is needed for publishing these facts, which, throughout the whole time of the Exhibition, strongly impressed all concerned in the management with the necessity of making similar provisions for the public wherever large numbers are congregated, and with the sufferings which must be endured by all, but more especially by females, on account of the want of them. These statements will also show that in England, as well as in France, such establishments may be made perfectly remunerative.

(*1st Report of the Commissioners of the Exhibition of 1851*, Parliamentary Papers 1852, vol. 26, Appendix 30.)

Profits were also made from catering. The Commissioners contracted out this task to Messrs. Schweppes who paid £5,500 for the privilege. By the end of the five months they had made a profit of some £45,000. The refreshments sold included:

Bread, Quarterns	52,094	Savoury patties	23,040 lbs
,, cottage loaves	60,698	Italian cakes	11,797
,, French rolls	7,617	Biscuits	37,300 lbs
Pound cakes	68,428	Bath buns	934,691
,, at 3d.	36,950	Plain buns	870,027
Savoury cakes	20,415	Banbury cakes	34,070
,, pies	33,456 lbs	Sausage rolls	28,046
Victoria biscuits	73,280	Mustard	1,120 lbs
Macaroons	1,500 lbs	Jellies	2,400 quarts
Rich cakes	2,280 lbs	Coffee	14,299 lbs
Pastry at 2d.	36,000	Tea	1,015 lbs
Schoolcakes	4,800	Chocolate	4,836 lbs
Preserved cherries, etc.	4,840 lbs	Milk	33,432 quarts
Pine apples	2,000	Cream	32,049 quarts
Pickles	1,046 gal.	Schweppes' Soda Water,	
Meat	113 tons	Lemonade &	
Potted meat,		Ginger Beer	1,092,337 bottles
tongues, etc.	36,130 lbs	Masters' Pear Syrup	5,350 bottles

| Hams | 33 tons | Rough ice | 363 tons |
| Potatoes | 36 tons | Salt | 37 tons |

(*1st Report of the Commissioners of the Exhibition of 1851*, Parliamentary Papers 1852, vol. 26, Appendix 29)

Virtually the only goods that weren't sold at the Exhibition were tobacco and alcoholic drink. The ban on alcohol was a manifestation of a growing temperance movement in the country but the main reason for no liquor was the fear of the working classes getting drunk and causing disturbances. But these fears were unfounded and behaviour overall was exemplary. During the whole period of the Exhibition, only 25 persons were prosecuted for offences committed inside the building.

5 AFTER THE EXHIBITION

It had always been recognized that Hyde Park would not be a permanent site for the Crystal Palace. But a building which had made such an impact on the public could not just be dismantled. In fact, it was bought by the London, Brighton and South Coast Railway for some £70,000 and moved to a site at Sydenham. The intention was that it should serve as a museum and a People's Palace, and with this in mind, the railway company laid a line from London Bridge to the grounds at Sydenham. Despite the efforts of Henry Mayhew and others who pleaded for Sunday openings, on the grounds that Sunday was the most convenient day for working class people to visit the Palace, the Sabbatarians were far more influential. Indeed, not only did they ensure that the Crystal Palace would not be open but in 1856 they were successful in obtaining the Sunday closure of the National Gallery and the British Museum.

Nevertheless, the Crystal Palace became the model for other entertainment centres and 'People's Palaces' at Alexandra Park and in the East End were built in the 1860s. Saturday concerts were also pioneered at the Crystal Palace and these proved to be particularly popular. The Palace also became famous for its triennial Handel festivals which started in 1857. It is interesting to note that it was these music and choral concerts which attracted the largest audiences for any organized leisure activity around this time. More than a quarter of a million attended the four festivals held between 1857 and 1865.

There were a number of proposals for how the profits from the Exhibition, which amounted to £186,000, should be spent. The prime aim was that the money should be used to further the Sciences and Arts. Eventually it was decided to spend some of the money to buy 70 acres of land opposite Hyde Park in South Kensington, on which museums and places of learning would be built. Accordingly, the Victoria and Albert Museum (originally called the South Kensington Museum — see television programme 27) was started in 1852, the Albert Hall in 1867 and the Natural History Museum in 1881.

One project on which Prince Albert, and Henry Cole in particular, wanted to spend some of the Exhibition's profits was the establishment of a technological university in London and the promotion of technical education for the working classes in the provinces by the setting up of a number of schools of science. Although the latter part of this scheme did not come to fruition, one immediate result of Cole's pressure was that the Department of Art became the Department of Science and Art, and in 1859 its examination system was instituted in science subjects so that in 1870 almost 30,000 students throughout the country were studying for these centrally organized examinations. By 1890, the number of students had risen to 134,000. After the Education Act of 1870 this Department of Art and Science was effectively the main government agency for secondary education throughout the country.

Cole's dream of a technological university which would also train teachers was slowly realized. He linked it with another project of his, the establishment of a patent museum, and eventually was able to build some laboratories on the South Kensington site. These were opened in 1872, forming the nucleus of the Normal School of Science, later the Royal College of Science, which became part of the Imperial College, established in 1902.

6 CONCLUSION

I want now to re-cap on the main features of Victorian society.

 Exercise

Look back over this unit and try to pick out what main points emerge about the nature of Victorian society at the time of the Great Exhibition (i.e. what kind of society do you think it was?)

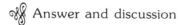 Answer and discussion

Britain was the leading industrial nation in the world in 1851 and this was reflected by a growing prosperity within the country. The organizers of the Exhibition were paying homage to British craftsmanship and to a society which believed in free competition, free trade and individual endeavour. They believed, however, that if Britain was to maintain its technological lead over the rest of the world, it would have to apply increasingly to all industries the new advances being made in scientific knowledge. They saw no reason why this should not happen and so they had a tremendous confidence in the future and a belief that if the nation's workforce remained industrious and if it was possible to attain peace and harmony, both at home and abroad, then there would be no limits to progress and technological advances.

Not all people shared this confidence. Despite these advances poverty had not been eliminated and, although the mechanization of industry enabled goods to be produced more cheaply and in greater quantities, there was a continued questioning of whether industrialization had been entirely beneficial. Living conditions in some of the new factory towns were squalid and some of the new industrial processes and the division of labour had made jobs monotonous and, in some people's eyes, dehumanizing. In addition, the use of new mechanical techniques was often misguided and was leading to an ornateness, ugliness and a debasement of art.

Again, although Victoria was the head of the established church and religion and although concern with morality seemed to loom large in the lives of many people (after all this was a period when there was a growth in both temperance and sabbatarian movements and respectability, with its constituents of hard work, self-education and a happy family life, were seemingly becoming increasingly important), nevertheless, the religious census revealed that many people were not church goers, and, in addition, drunkenness and gambling were still major social problems.

I have purposely kept this discussion short because later units will examine all these problems in much greater detail. It would be wrong even at this stage to over-simplify the picture of Britain in 1851 as a confident society firmly believing in progress, work and peace. It will be up to you to come to your own conclusions as you look at the development of British society and the arts in the period between the Great Exhibition and 1890.

PART II   RE-READING 'HARD TIMES'

You should spend the rest of this week's study re-reading *Hard Times*. Remember that, if necessary, you have discussion of the novel in the *Study Guide to Charles Dickens's 'Hard Times'* and in section 5 of Units 4–6. It is important to re-read *Hard Times* now as it is an essential element of your study of Victorian Britain in the second part of the course.

Unit 17

INTERDISCIPLINARY STUDY: AN INTRODUCTION

Contributors

Arthur Marwick has written sections 1–4, assisted by Michael Rossington, Richard Middleton, Gill Perry, Stuart Brown, and Gerrylyn Roberts. Section 5 was written by Nicola Durbridge.

SET READING

As you work through Unit 17 you will need to refer to

Geoffrey Best (1979) *Mid-Victorian Britain 1851–75* (Set Book)

Charles Dickens (1989 edition) *Hard Times* (Set Book)

John Golby (ed.) (1986) *Culture and Society in Britain 1850–1890* (Course Reader)

Units 1–3 *Introduction to History*

CASSETTE

Cassette 4, side 1, band 1 *Writing an Interdisciplinary Essay*

AIM

The overall aim of this unit is to show you how the introductions to the individual disciplines in the first part of the course, and the detailed studies of Unit 16, can be brought together to enable you, in the second part of the course, to carry out an interdisciplinary study of 'Culture and Society in Britain 1850–90'.

OBJECTIVES

After completing this unit:

1   you should have brought together in the forefront of your mind key points relating to Victorian society raised in the previous units, particularly in Units 1–3 and in Unit 16;

2   you should be clear about which of the concepts and approaches that link the different disciplines together will be necessary for the interdisciplinary study which makes up the remainder of the course;

3   you should understand why interdisciplinary approaches are essential for a proper study of 'Culture and Society in Britain 1850–90', and why ten major interdisciplinary topics have been selected to make this study possible.

4   you should gain a preliminary understanding of why scholars sometimes use such phrases as 'dominant ideology' and 'cultural consumption' and of the manner in which you yourself will be expected to use them.

The first section of this unit corresponds with the first objective stated above, the second and third sections with the second objective, and the fourth section with the third objective. The fourth objective is dealt with within sub-section 4.5 in section 4. At the end of the unit there is a special indexing exercise (devised by Nicola Durbridge) to help you find your way through the ten topics as you study Units 18–32. This, therefore, is a (deliberately) short unit, enabling you to get ahead with your tutor-marked assignment. You should also take the opportunity to be sure that you have read properly the chapters by Thompson and Bédarida in the Supplementary Material booklet.

1 REVISION OF BASIC POINTS ABOUT VICTORIAN SOCIETY

The material particularly relevant to the interdisciplinary study of Victorian society you have now embarked upon is as follows:

1 The historical outline of Victorian society provided in Unit 1 (and the accompanying *Chronology*) and discussed throughout Units 1–3; and other aspects of Victorian society which have been discussed in Units 4–15 (for example, Victorian poetry, Victorian painting, utilitarianism).

2 Your reading and re-reading of *Hard Times*.

3 The discussion of the Great Exhibition contained in Unit 16.

You will remember that in Unit 1, section 5, I suggested six headings under which we could summarize the 'essential features' of Victorian society:

1 Basic features of the economy: industrial, agricultural, commercial sources of wealth; general sense of economic boom.

2 Social condition: rising profits and wages, but gross inequalities and deep pools of misery.

3 Town and country: growing industrialization but continuing importance of the countryside.

4 Industrialization and the social structure: 'classes' and 'orders' or 'estates', new *life styles*, growth of mass sport, for example, football.

5 Culture and belief: prudishness, importance of religion, thrift, private enterprise, yet ambiguities and paradoxes; belief and unbelief; optimism and insecurity; pacifism and patriotism; utilitarianism and sentiment; autocracy and democracy.

6 The major changes in Victorian society from the 1870s onwards. Did optimism give way to pessimism? Was there a 'consensus' (in social attitude, beliefs and so on) in mid-Victorian society which was replaced by new stresses and strains, and new social criticism?

You were also provided with a basic chronology of the main political, economic, cultural and religious events. Remember that Television programme 1 *The Necessity for History* made some useful points about Victorian attitudes and values.

I now want you to have beside you Units 1–3, *Hard Times*, Geoffrey Best's *Mid-Victorian Britain 1851–75*, and your Course Reader. I am going to fire some questions at you in order to remind you of points that we studied at the beginning of the course; each question will be related to the headings I have just listed. At this point only very brief answers are required.

 Exercise

1 (a) Turn to the tables on pages 99–100 of Best. What were the major sources of (i) employment and (ii) national income in 1851, and what major changes took place between 1851 and 1881?

(b) From which source, or sources, did Mr Bounderby derive his wealth? (If you cannot answer from memory, turn to page 18 of *Hard Times*.)

2 Turn to Best, pages 111–19. What is Professor Best's view about wages in the period 1850–75?

3 Where did the majority of British people live in 1851, and how did this differ from 1841? (If in doubt, turn to Best and the table on page 24.)

4 Recalling the discussion in Units 1–3, what is the difference between, on the one side, *classes*, and on the other, *orders* or *estates*?

5   (a) Turn to extract II.4 in the Course Reader, 'Letter from Charles Darwin to Asa Gray, 22 May 1860'. What important aspect of Victorian attitudes does this illuminate?

(b) In what sense is Chapter 1 of *Hard Times* a critique of utilitarianism? Is it a fair critique?

6   Read this passage from *Hard Times* then answer the questions that follow.

'But, if you please, Miss Louisa,' Sissy pleaded, 'I am − O so stupid!'
Louisa, with a brighter laugh than usual, told her she would be wiser by-and-by.
'You don't know,' said Sissy, half crying, 'what a stupid girl I am. All through school hours I make mistakes. Mr and Mrs M'Choakumchild call me up, over and over again, regularly to make mistakes. I can't help them. They seem to come natural to me.'
'Mr and Mrs M'Choakumchild never make any mistakes themselves, I suppose, Sissy?'
'O no!' she eagerly returned. 'They know everything.'
'Tell me some of your mistakes.'
'I am almost ashamed,' said Sissy, with reluctance. 'But today, for instance, Mr M'Choakumchild was explaining to us about Natural Prosperity.'
'National, I think it must have been,' observed Louisa.
'Yes, it was. − But isn't it the same?' she timidly asked.
'You had better say, National, as he said so,' returned Louisa, with her dry reserve.
'National Prosperity. And he said, Now, this schoolroom is a Nation. And in this nation, there are fifty millions of money. Isn't this a prosperous nation? Girl number twenty, isn't this a prosperous nation, and a'n't you in a thriving state?'
'What did you say?' asked Louisa.
'Miss Louisa, I said I didn't know. I thought I couldn't know whether it was a prosperous nation or not, and whether I was in a thriving state or not, unless I knew who had got the money, and whether any of it was mine. But that had nothing to do with it. It was not in the figures at all,' said Sissy, wiping her eyes.
'That was a great mistake of yours,' observed Louisa.
'Yes, Miss Louisa, I know it was, now. Then Mr M'Choakumchild said he would try me again. And he said, This schoolroom is an immense town, and in it there are a million of inhabitants, and only five-and-twenty are starved to death in the streets, in the course of a year. What is your remark on that proportion? And my remark was − for I couldn't think of a better one − that I thought it must be just as hard upon those who were starved, whether the others were a million, or a million million. And that was wrong, too.'
'Of course it was.'

(a) Where does this passage come in the novel, and who are the characters mentioned in it? (This is not a terribly important question, but you might as well answer it.)
(b) (This is the more important question.) Does the general view of mid-Victorian society presented by Dickens in this passage coincide or disagree with that derived from your study of the Great Exhibition?

7   What major development in the economy did contemporaries feel was affecting them from 1873 onwards?

8   Give the dates of the two major parliamentary Reform Acts in the period, and quickly state which sections of society they extended the franchise to.

Specimen answers and discussion

1   (a) In 1851, 32.7 per cent of the occupied population were employed in manufacture, with 20.9 per cent still employed in agriculture; the next biggest area of employment was domestic service, 13.3 per cent. By 1881 the percentage in agriculture has dropped significantly to 11.5; the percentage in manufacture has actually gone down very slightly, as the percentages in

'dealing', transport, public and professional service, and so on, have moved up. When we look at national income, trade and transport are seen to have a much more significant role: 18.7 per cent in 1851 and 23 per cent in 1881. But the major source of income is mining, manufacturing, building, with 34.2 per cent in 1851 and 37.6 per cent in 1881. Meantime the agriculture figures echo those in the previous table: 20.3 per cent in 1851 but only 10.4 per cent in 1881.

(b) We are told: 'He was a rich man: banker, merchant, manufacturer, and what not.' Thus, his wealth was both industrial and commercial. (It is fairly clear from the rest of the book that 'what not' did not include ownership of land.)

2   In contrast to some other commentators, Best is very cautious, explaining the difficulties in getting exact figures. He is not prepared to commit himself to a general rise in wages before the 1870s. For the early part of the period, he feels that rising wages for the more prosperous members of the working class were not incompatible with continuing low wages for the depressed masses.

3   According to the 1851 census a majority of the population (54 per cent) was living in towns, but this, it is always important to note, includes small towns as well as large towns; in 1841 only 48.3 per cent of the population had been living in towns.

4   Orders or estates are the basis of social structure in pre-industrial society: classes come in with industrialization, but it is important to remember that social structure in mid-Victorian society was still something of a mixture of classes and estates.

5   (a) A deep reluctance to abandon religious belief despite the scientific evidence.

(b) The central core of utilitarianism lay in the principle of the greatest happiness of the greatest number rather than in a stress on facts as such, so if this is a critique of utilitarianism, it is of a rather simplified and distorted version of that philosophy. Many Victorians who believed in rigorous attention to scientific evidence were not utilitarians. Much of the very real progress in Victorian society depended upon rational scientific attitudes. Thus the opening chapter, though powerful as a critique of a particular narrow attitude of mind lacking humanity and romance, is scarcely fair as an indictment of utilitarianism or, more generally, of the scientific outlook.

There is much room for argument here and I do not, of course expect you to have said exactly what I have said. The main point to remember is that utilitarianism is something rather different from mere insistence on the supremacy of 'facts'.

6   (a) The episode takes place soon after Sissy Jupe, daughter of a circus performer, has been brought into the Gradgrind household. Miss Louisa is Gradgrind's sixteen-year-old daughter. Mr and Mrs M'Choakumchild are teachers at a school patronized by Gradgrind and Bounderby.

(b) There is only a conflict, I think, if you take *Hard Times* as always standing for poverty and insecurity, and the Great Exhibition as always standing for prosperity and optimism. In fact, in this passage, we hear of Mr M'Choakumchild discussing national prosperity, the very background and occasion for the Great Exhibition. In the discussion of the Great Exhibition you learned that there were critics of it, particularly of its emphasis on vulgar prosperity. The point in the Dickens passage, of course, is that no amount of national prosperity can lessen the impact, for those involved, of starving to death in the streets. Thus, in that this passage does bring out that there was a great contemporary preoccupation with, and pride in, national prosperity (even if Dickens himself is critical of this attitude), it complements what you learn from your study of the Great Exhibition, rather than contradicting it.

7   'The Great Depression'.

8   The Reform Act of 1867 which extended the franchise in urban areas; the Reform Act of 1884 which extended the franchise in country areas.

2 TEXTS AND ARGUMENTS: REVISION OF THE FIRST PART OF THE COURSE WITH RESPECT TO ITS RELEVANCE TO THE SECOND PART

Among a number of things that you learned in studying the different individual disciplines was how to analyse different kinds of 'text' (that is to say, historical documents, poems or novels, individual paintings, pieces of music, philosophical arguments). In the second part of the course you will be going on to develop arguments about Culture and Society, The Impact of Science, Town and Country in later nineteenth-century Britain, etc., etc. In order to be able to develop arguments you have to be able to refer to precise pieces of evidence, or, in other words, 'texts': you can't, for example, argue about Tennyson's relationship to the rest of Victorian culture, or to religious ideas, or whatever, without first being familiar with some of Tennyson's poems ('texts'). Thus, the skills you have learned in analysing different types of texts will continue to be very important in the second part of the course, where you have some very rich collections of texts to work on: the Course Reader, the *Illustration Booklet*, and the five volumes of texts particularly designed for Summer School use, but which can also be used in your general studies.

This very important link between the first and second parts of the course forms a framework both for your work at Summer School and for the tasks you have to demonstrate you can do in the examination. Your first five short tutorials at Summer School will be concerned with the five individual disciplines, with an emphasis on textual analysis. You will then have five individual days on the interdisciplinary topics belonging to the second part of the course in which you will be developing practice in applying evidence to the solving of problems and the developing of arguments. Part I of the exam consists of single discipline textual analysis; Part II of interdisciplinary essay questions relating to Britain 1850–1890.

I am now going to give you five text-based questions, similar to the ones you will meet in Part I of the exam (there may be slight variations from year to year in the exact phrasing and format). I want you to write down an answer to each one: I will then discuss possible answers with you, pointing out their relevance to the sort of arguments you will be expected to be able to advance during your study of the second part of the course.

 Exercise

Question 1   History

Carefully read the following extract which is from the Minutes of Evidence to the Royal Commission on Trades Unions, 1867, published in *Parliamentary Papers*, 1868: first the Chairman, then Mr Roebuck, a member of the Commission, are questioning Mr William Allan, Secretary of the Amalgamated Society of Engineers.

Chairman: What have been the grounds or causes of such disputes as you have had in the trade within the last 10 years?

Mr Allan: They have principally arisen from piecework and the large number of boys employed.

Chairman: They have been, then, I understand, for the purpose of enforcing or maintaining trade rules?

Mr Allan: Yes, regulating the trade.

Chairman: Have they been for the most part to introduce new rules or to maintain those already existing?

Mr Allan: To maintain existing rules and customs . . .

Mr Roebuck: Will you explain what the dispute was in reference to boys being employed?

Mr Allan: That they were introduced in a larger proportion than what the trade recognizes.

Mr Roebuck: What do you mean when you speak of what the trade recognizes, in the introduction of boys?

Mr Allan: It depends on the class of work. For instance, in an engine factory very few boys are employed in comparison with the number of men. In machine shops and tool-making establishments there are a large number employed, and in some instances they have introduced boys to what we think an alarming extent, and the result is that the men have objected to it.

Mr Roebuck: Could the boys do the work of the men?

Mr Allan: They might be capable of doing a portion of it.

Mr Roebuck: And did the masters think they could?

Mr Allan: I have no doubt they did, or else they would not have employed them.

Mr Roebuck: Why should you prevent a master from employing boys who can do the work?

Mr Allan: We have a perfect right to say to him 'if you employ a certain number of boys beyond what we conceive to be a proper number, we will not work for you'.

Mr Roebuck: A proper number means the number that you like?

Mr Allan: What the men think right.

Imagine you are writing a history of British Trade Unions, 1850—1890, and wish to make use of this extract. In the form of a brief essay (*not* notes) discuss the points listed below. *DO NOT simply write a general answer on source criticism.*

1   What kind of *primary* source this is.

2   What problems need sorting out before you can make full use of this source.

3   What limitations, weaknesses and strengths it has as a source for 'British Trade Unions 1850—1890'.

4   What you learn from it (distinguishing between the witting and unwitting testimony).

Question 2   Literature

Read the following poem, three or four times, then write an essay in answer to the question which follows:

Hap

If but some vengeful god would call to me
From up the sky, and laugh: 'Thou suffering thing,
Know that thy sorrow is my ecstasy,
That thy love's loss is my hate's profiting!'

Then would I bear it, clench myself, and die,   *5*
Steeled by the sense of ire unmerited;
Half-eased in that a Powerfuller than I
Had willed and meted[1] me the tears I shed.

But not so. How arrives it joy lies slain,
And why unblooms the best hope ever sown?   *10*
 — Crass Casualty[2] obstructs the sun and rain,
And dicing Time for gladness casts a moan . . .
These purblind[3] Doomsters had as readily strown
Blisses about my pilgrimage as pain.

Thomas Hardy

[1] Apportioned, allotted.
[2] Insensible chance.
[3] Partly blind, dim-sighted.

How does the language of the poem convey its meaning and effect? (You should consider the way rhyme, rhythm, alliteration, imagery and unexpected words and turns of phrase variously contribute to this.)

Question 3   Music

Listen to Sir Arthur Sullivan's song 'The Lost Chord'. (It may be found on Cassette 1, side 1, band 7, and the words are printed in *Cassette Notes 1*. In what ways has Sullivan used the various elements of music to express the meaning of the words?

Question 4   Art History

Look at the following illustrations in the *Illustration Booklet:*

Colour Plate 11   Thomas Gainsborough, *Mr and Mrs Andrews*, c. 1749, oil on canvas, 70 × 120 cm, National Gallery, London.

Colour Plate 35   William Holman Hunt, *The Hireling Shepherd*, 1851−2, oil on canvas, 76 × 110 cm, Manchester City Art Galleries.

Compare the treatment of genre in these two pictures. Paying particular attention to the conventions of the genre and the mode of representation, discuss how meaning is constructed in each of the works.

   (You may find that Gombrich's notion of 'schemata' and the 'beholder's share', and the ways in which these operate in representation will help you to consider how meaning is constructed in the works. Remember also to take into account the information in the captions.)

Question 5   Philosophy

Study the following passage carefully and answer the questions that relate to it:

By the publication of Sir J.C.Hippisley's work on Prison Discipline, the public attention has been called to the mischievous effects of a punishment which has been hailed as the great modern improvement in penal legislation — the Tread Wheel.

   There are strong objections to the employment of labour, in any case, as a punishment. If we consider from what causes men are induced to commit that species of crimes which are most common — petty violations of property — it will be found that in the great majority of cases, it is *aversion to labour* which has been the operating motive. To prevent crime, means ought to be taken to counteract the painful associations which give rise to this aversion. For such a purpose no contrivance can be worse chosen than that of forcing labour, and that of the severest kind, upon the offender as a punishment.

   When a poor man is at large, earning his bread by his exertions, unless his labour be excessive, there are many circumstances which tend to make it agreeable to him. It is to labour that he owes all the comforts and enjoyments of existence. By labour alone can he hope to advance himself in life and raise the prospects of his family. All this has not been sufficient to counteract his habits of indolence for those habits have prevailed, and instead of labouring he has turned thief; and yet in order to cure him of his aversion to labour, he is placed in a situation where, instead of being the source of his enjoyments, it becomes an engine of unrequited misery to him, and of misery of the most intense description.

This objection applies strongly to all kinds of labour, when considered merely as a punishment; but most of all, to the tread-mill, the horrors of which, as described by Sir John Cox Hippisley, appear unequalled in the modern annals of *legalized* torture.

(From 'Tread Wheel', From a Correspondent [J. S. Mill], *Globe and Traveller*, 3 Oct. 1823.)

1   Why is the objection given by the author to the use of employment as a means of punishment intended to apply 'most of all' to the tread-mill?

2   What assumptions does the author make in putting forward this objection?

3   What evidence can you find in the passage that the author is a utilitarian?

 Specimen answer

Question 1

This is a public document of record, transcribing verbatim the evidence given by expert witnesses to a commission of enquiry, or an official investigation (any indication along these lines would be acceptable to your examiner).

It is always important to understand any technical or archaic terms as contemporaries would have understood them: thus, among problems to be sorted out would be the age group covered by the term 'boys', the exact meaning of 'piecework', and what is meant by 'what the trade recognizes' (it means, of course, what the *unions* recognize). Larger problems are that we need an immense amount more in the way of context: the rest of the Royal Commission Report, the circumstances in which the report was set up, the nature of the Amalgamated Society of Engineers compared with other unions, what the class background and attitudes of the Royal Commission (and, in this particular case of the Chairman and Mr Roebuck) were.

The main limitations are that this extract is only one small part of only one document, and that it refers only to a part of the period, the fifteen years prior to 1867 (and thus is of no use to the period 1867–1890). The weaknesses are that we have here only the evidence of one man, and one union, and also that the matters discussed are very much limited to the questions the Commission decides to ask. Members of the Commission will no doubt have their own vested interests, and clearly the witness will reply in a manner as favourable as possible to the interests of his own union. Against that, it can be argued that this extract does form part of a systematic enquiry dedicated, according to its lights, to establishing the 'truth': the question-and-answer method should be a good one for getting at that 'truth'. The strength, indeed, is that this extract is from a public document of record open to scrutiny and subject to high standards of accuracy and objectivity. Furthermore, we are actually getting the direct testimony of a trade-union leader who must know what he is talking about. We can have a reasonable expectation that the facts will be accurate, and certainly it is a great strength in the document that it gives direct insights into attitudes and assumptions of the time.

The *witting* testimony is that the main causes of industrial disputes in the last ten years have been over piecework and over the employment of boys, that this trade union has certain 'trade rules' on these matters and that industrial action has been on the basis of maintaining these. We learn that, in accordance with the existing customs, different proportions of boys are employed in different spheres, very few in an engine factory, quite a large number in machine shops and tool-making establishments. We learn that there is acceptance on both sides that at least a proportion of this work can actually be done by boys. We learn that the union sanction against practices that violate existing rules and customs is withdrawal of labour.

Unwittingly, we learn that there seems to be no moral objection on either side to the employment of boys: the union concern is purely with actual numbers. There seems to be a kind of shared perception that employers are entitled to get away with what they can, and it is up to the union to resist in what it perceives as a defence of its own interests. Within that consensus, it is clear that masters and workers are seen to have opposed interests, and it is for the union, as appropriate, to take industrial action. It is clear that the Chairman and Mr Roebuck on behalf of the Commission see the unions as occupying a somewhat autocratic role, while the unions operate on the basis that they represent what their men think (this comes out in the final question and answer). It seems that basic questions of wages and hours as such are not major sources of conflict: this would suggest a certain stability in relations between union and masters, although of course piecework and employment of boys are issues which do relate to earnings. Finally, this extract does provide unwitting evidence of a quite high level of education on the part of the trade-union leader Mr Allan (he is certainly, at the very least, very articulate).

Discussion

Don't worry if you didn't come up with all these points. But I hope you will begin to see the point of doing this kind of exercise if I tell you that one of the topics for discussion in the second part of the course is 'Working-Class Organization and Culture'. In developing arguments around that topic you might well want to use extracts like this one. Before you can make use of it you have to assess both its limits and its strengths, just as we have been doing here. What it directly says (the witting testimony) is pretty clear: but you can see from my answer how much, much more you can get from a historical document once you learn how, as it were, 'to read between the lines', to bring out the assumptions that lie behind what is being said. I think my final point is a particularly good one, using this document to suggest that a trade-union leader could be quite literate and articulate. However, there are always dangers in pushing unwitting testimony too far: it is always just possible that Mr Allan's language and grammar were tidied up before the report was published. We certainly don't expect *you* to know all the answers: what we do want you to be able to do is to show that you can approach a document critically and intelligently, assess its usefulness to you, and then be able to bring out clearly what you do learn from it.

Specimen answer

Question 2

First, a few general words on 'meaning and effect'. The title, 'Hap', meaning chance or luck, informs the reader of the basic argument; that the forces governing mankind are indifferent to its suffering. The poem expresses scepticism towards religious faith, and takes the form of the speaker engaging meditatively on two different explanations of how human existence is governed.

The rhyme scheme abab, cdcd, *efeffe*, and particularly the 'closure' effect with the reversal of rhymes at the end gives the poem a sense of strict formality (this conforms, though in a slightly irregular way, to 'sonnet form'). But the poem derives its powerful, suggestive effect from its unexpected words and phrases, eg., 'a Powerfuller', 'unblooms', 'Crass Casualty', 'purblind Doomsters'.

The language of the first two relatively straightforward stanzas dramatizes an ironic position with regard to religious faith of a conventional kind. By imagining 'some vengeful god' delighting in our suffering then we could at least be relieved by the knowledge that the injustice of our suffering was the result of the cruelty of an individual who had control over our destinies ('a Powerfuller than I/Had willed and meted me the tears I shed.') The irony of these lines lies in the evident pleasure that is gained from this rational explanation ('Steeled by the sense of ire unmerited;/Half-eased in that . . .') Hardy mixes a tone of speculative intellectual detachment ('If but') with one of high drama which is almost comical: the god calling 'to me/From up the sky'; 'Then would I bear it, clench myself and die'.

The change of tempo and rhythm in the first two lines of the last stanza signals a rejection of this absurd, but tempting, fantasy. There is a bleak despondency here which the language carries: 'And why unblooms the best hope ever sown?' The imagery of this line suggests the decay of a flower, and implicitly the destructive power of nature. The last four lines are difficult. Hardy personifies Chance as indifferent rather than malevolent, at odds with Nature and therefore with humankind; 'Crass Casualty obstructs the sun and rain'. The following line is the most difficult in the poem: 'And dicing Time for gladness casts a moan . . .'. This presumably means that Chance ('Crass Casualty'), even when it gambles with Time to 'throw' (i.e. make) happiness, often 'throws' despair, i.e. loses instead ('casts a moan'). The final couplet emphasizes the indifference of these blind Fates of chance ('purblind Doomsters') to the speaker's own condition, since they could have as well made him happy as sad ('had as readily strown/Blisses about my pilgrimage as pain').

Effect and meaning are reinforced by the way in which the poem moves from a mood of ironic satisfaction, dramatically represented in one scenario, to quiet despondency as a result of recognizing the conclusive evidence of the other.

 Discussion

Again, I can imagine that your answer may have varied quite widely from that. A literary text, in any case, will provide for a much wider range of perfectly respectable responses, than will a historical document (the fourth line of the last stanza is particularly hard to interpret and there is no harm in admitting this). But the two crucial points to emerge from this exercise are:

1   You really must grasp the content, theme, and meaning of a poem, something that will take several very careful readings; it simply is not good enough to have some vague general impression as to what the poem is about.

2   You have to develop an understanding of the way in which *language* (rhyme, alliteration, unexpected phrases, etc.) is used to convey meaning and effect.

In developing arguments in the second part of the course you will frequently wish to refer to poems you have read − but before you can make use of them you will have to be able to carry out this kind of analysis.

 Specimen answer

Question 3

The words seem to be about the rather mysterious power of music to console us in the worries of *everyday* life, to bring a kind of spiritual peace into mundane anxieties. The steady tempo and very simple, regular rhythmic patterns establish a basic tranquillity, and the tune, with its mainly stepwise movements, and numerous repeated pitches, amplifies this mood. The chords which support the tune are mainly simple too, and the progressions have a hymn-like quality. Indeed, the tempo, rhythm, tune and harmonies, altogether, create a sort of hymn-tune effect; this is especially striking at such points as 'But I struck one chord of music, like the sound of a great Amen'. The piano introduction, coda and interlude between verses one and two also sound 'churchy', partly because of the kind of chords that are used, but also because of the use of contrapuntal imitation. On the whole, the texture of the piano accompaniment is rich, with full chords (a church organ effect?). For verse two, however, Sullivan expresses the 'calm', 'quiet', and 'peace' mentioned in the words, and possibly the angel's role as well, by shifting the accompaniment into a higher register. And the climax of the song, in verse four, as the poet anticipates the glorious music of heaven, is created through chords even bigger spread and richer than in verse one, together with a rise in the dynamic level. The only marked interruption to the basic mood comes in verse three where a more insistent rhythm with quicker notes in the piano, a change of tonality (to a minor key) and some more dissonant chords produce an effective setting of the anguish of the words 'I have sought, but I seek it vainly . . .'

 Discussion

I won't repeat my general point about the need for comprehension and analysis before you can begin to make use of a musical text. Here, with respect to the second part of the course, the obvious point is the usefulness of a text like this, and such analysis of it, to understanding the importance of religion to the Victorians. Here it is (as quite often) conditioning the style of a secular song in quite specific stylistic, as well as general emotional, ways. In much Victorian culture there is a tendency to 'diffusive Christianity', a vague but pervasive spiritual ambience (rather than precise theological or liturgical affiliations).

 Specimen answer

Question 4

An important issue to address here is how to classify these works according to genre. Neither painting fits clearly into any single category of genre. They are of similar size, and initially both entered private collections. The Gainsborough, although a commissioned portrait, combines the conventions of portraiture with those of landscape painting (Mr and Mrs Andrews occupy only about one-third of the total composition). *The Hunt*, on the other hand, is related to the traditions of Victorian *genre painting* (i.e. the portrayal of everyday life). It could also be argued, however, that the religious symbolism of the work functions as a moralizing narrative, which was reminiscent of the conventions of history painting, as is the title, taken from a song in Shakespeare's *King Lear*. Although the superficial subject-matter of *The Hireling Shepherd* is a man and a woman in a landscape, it is clearly *not* a commissioned portrait group in the manner of the Gainsborough. In fact *The Hireling Shepherd* actually reworks a well established art-historical theme, that of pastoral scenes of shepherds and shepherdesses which had already become popular in the eighteenth century.
   The representation of landscape contributes significantly to the meanings conveyed in each painting. Gainsborough was following an eighteenth-century tradition of representing the patron in relation to his/her estate or grounds, although the dominance of the landscape in his work was unusual. He depicts a fertile estate with fields full of freshly harvested sheaths of corn, a landscape which could be seen to contribute to the image of a proud and affluent landowner. In the Hunt the landscape is full of religious symbolism (e.g. the straying sheep who have eaten spoilt wheat and become 'blown'), all of which contribute to a system of symbolic references for which his work was renowned. The relationship of the landscape to the figure group in each painting also contributes to the possible meanings conveyed. In the Gainsborough the relatively stiff portrait group to one side of the composition emphasizes the sitter's role as landowner, as does the faithful dog and squire-like pose. Despite their apparent informality the shepherd and shepherdess in the Hunt form a central triangular group, and a narrative focus for the various symbolic references and incidents which are represented throughout the composition. These elements are all part of the 'schemata' or modes of representation employed by each artist, as is the minutely detailed Pre-Raphaelite technique and heightened colour of *The Hireling Shepherd*, which contrasts with the Dutch-influenced naturalism of the Gainsborough. As you will find out when you come to Unit 22, in 1852 several reviewers described Hunt's figures as

'coarse', 'ill-washed' labourers. The directness of his style seemed to upset traditional conventions for representing pastoral scenes. In this sense the 'beholders'' expectations of how a pastoral scene should be painted helped to produce a critical reading of *The Hireling Shepherd*. In terms of its contemporary reception, it is worth mentioning that the Hunt invited several controversial readings, including the view that this work revealed High Church sympathies. Thus a range of meanings were read into the work, meanings which often revealed the interests and assumption of the critics involved.

 Discussion

It's unlikely that you will have done such a comprehensive answer as that. Once you had got to the exam we would expect you to be able to bring in information from Unit 22 – but sometimes the paintings in the exam will be unseen and then we will not expect detailed information about 'reception', etc.

What I want to stress here is how this exercise brings out the significance of 'schemata' or 'modes of representation'. Remember from your reading of Gombrich not to fall into the error of thinking that a painting is an exact version of reality: painters already have certain 'schemata' in mind which affects the way in which they represent their subject-matter. It is terribly important to give very careful attention to this question of 'representation' – as must be very apparent to you from the 'model answer' you have just read. In your arguments and discussions in the interdisciplinary part of the course you will frequently wish to refer to paintings (yet another kind of text) – but first you will need to have done the kind of analysis exemplified in this exercise.

The way in which some of these ideas relate to the second part of the course is discussed in section 4 of the *Study Guide to Gombrich's 'Art and Illusion'*. Please read this section now.

 Specimen answer

Question 5

1   The author's objection is that aversion to labour is the commonest cause of crime and that this aversion is the result of the 'painful associations' that labour has come to have for individuals who turn to crime. These associations can only be counteracted by experiences that will make labour more agreeable. But such better associations will not result from any form of forced labour and indeed the more severe such labour is, the more counter-productive it will be from the point of view of reducing the motive to crime. The tread-mill, by turning labour into a form of torture, is 'most of all' open to this objection, according to the author.

2   The author's assumptions, in putting forward this argument, include:

(a)   that the purpose of any mode of punishment is the prevention of crime;

(b)   that this is done by combating the motives to crime;

(c)   that the motive to crime in most cases is an aversion to labour;

(d)   that forced labour, in proportion to its unpleasantness, only increases the aversion to labour.

3   The evidence in the passage that its author was a utilitarian includes the following assumptions:

(a)   that people pursue what is pleasant and avoid what is unpleasant;

(b)   that the infliction of 'misery' can only be justified as a means to a greater good;

(c)   that punishment has no value in itself but is justifiable, if at all, because it produces good effects (e.g. less crime).

Discussion

Philosophical argument is often quite difficult to follow. The first purpose of an exercise of this sort is to find out if you can in fact puzzle out a philosophical argument and see exactly what it is the author is saying (often students jump at a passage like this and vaguely repeat some of the things that are being said without really having any clear idea of what the argument is and what conclusions it is coming to: you have to be able to read and *understand*). Secondly, this exercise tests your knowledge of utilitarianism, an important philosophical school which appears in both parts of the course.

3 REVISION OF MAIN INTERDISCIPLINARY CONCEPTS AND APPROACHES MENTIONED IN THE FIRST PART OF THE COURSE

Here are some more questions to jog your memory.

 Exercise

1   Serious study of the individual arts disciplines and of the interdisciplinary topic 'Culture and Society in Britain 1850–90', as you have just seen, involves the critical reading of 'texts'. What four activities (however different in detail) are common to the reading of all types of texts? (In the units introducing the different disciplines the points have been made using slightly different words, so it does not matter how you express your answer as long as you get the essential points.)

2   What are the three main ways in which 'culture' can be defined?

3   The second part of this course, which you are now embarked on, is entitled 'Culture and Society in Britain 1850–90'. Which meaning of 'culture' must be intended here?

4   From time to time throughout Units 1–15 mention was made of art,literature, and so on, as being 'culturally constructed'. What is meant by this phrase?

5   Are there any ways in which art, literature, music, and so on, can legitimately be perceived as being 'autonomous'?

6   In the arts generally what is the basic relationship between content, form and meaning?

 Specimen answer and discussion

1   (a) You have, first of all, to decide what category the text falls into: is it a novel or poem, and what type of novel or poem; is it a statue or painting, and what kind of painting, a 'public painting', a miniature, or what? Your reading will be affected by the category to which you assign the text.

(b)   You have to understand what it is you are reading (in the non-technical sense of the term), looking at, or listening to. Graham Martin stressed this particularly in regard to poems, where it is very important first of all to get the literal meaning. But, similarly, if you do not know what, in the simplest sense,

40

is depicted in a painting, you are not going to be able to make much of an analysis of it. This was not one of the first points I made with regard to a historical document, but I did stress that you have to understand the document as contemporaries would have understood it. In philosophy, quite clearly, you have to make a definite effort to understand the arguments which are being put forward in a piece of philosophical writing. Perhaps the processes are slightly different with music, but even here you have to listen and take in what it is you are hearing before you can proceed to any kind of analysis.

(c)   It is then that we come to what has been variously described as 'criticism', or 'doing analysis'. The techniques vary with the different disciplines, but the fundamental point of disciplined critical analysis is the same. You do not just, to put it in the most banal way, say 'very nice', or 'I do not like it', or 'I do not agree'. In all the different texts you will be looking at in Units 18–32 you will need to be analytical and critical.

(d)   You may not have made this as a separate point because, in fact, it is a kind of special extension of the process of criticism and analysis. This is the point that you have to pick up on allusions and references within your various texts. Whether they are references to classical mythology, hidden quotations from say, other composers or poets, developments of philosophical positions adopted by previous philosophers, or allusions to other historical events or characters (you may remember Macaulay's references to the 1848 revolutions and to Sir Robert Peel), you need to understand them fully before you can complete your analysis and criticism of the text.

2   The three definitions are:

(a)   The total network of human activities and value systems in a given society (the anthropological definition).

(b)   All the artistic and intellectual products and activities in a given society (to include sport, popular culture, and so on).

(c)   The 'best' artistic and intellectual products and activities in a given society (for example, 'classical' music, 'serious' literature).

This matter will be taken up again in Unit 22. If you are in any doubt, go back to the discussion in Unit 3, section 4.

3   Quite clearly the first definition cannot be intended, for in this definition 'society' and 'culture' come very near to meaning the same thing. What must be intended is the relationship between society on the one side and its 'creative products' on the other side. Thus, either definition (b) or (c) must be intended. In fact, part of the point of the second part of the course is that whereas today we would tend to look towards definition (b) with its inclusion of popular culture, sport, and so on, the Victorians themselves, with their rather snobbish attitudes, tended to concentrate on definition (c). If you opted for either definition (b) or definition (c) you were doing very well. But if you had difficulty with this question, look again at Unit 3, section 4.

4   When one says that the work of art is 'culturally constructed' one is saying that it is not the product of individual genius operating totally independently of social and cultural forces ('culture' in the first, social or anthropological definition), but that its nature is determined by the total complex cultural network. However, within that broadly agreed definition academics can mean rather different things when they use the phrase 'culturally constructed'. Some see the 'culture' as being of relatively short duration, and being distinctly different from other cultural periods; thus they might speak of 'capitalist culture' or 'bourgeois culture' with a life of, say, about a hundred years, or of 'Victorian culture', with a still shorter life. Others, however, might speak of 'Western culture' which allows for a work of art at any point in time being subject to influences which might go back many centuries. In section 6 of Unit 3 I suggested that a distinction might be drawn between speaking of the social or

historical context for a shorter time period, and using the phrase 'culturally constructed' for the much longer time period, but this would be by no means a universally agreed procedure. Anyway, if in your answer you got as far as my first sentence, that is excellent. The other points are matters for further debate and discussion.

5   In his discussion of 'Composer and Audience' in Units 7−9, Donald J. Burrows suggested that Beethoven had considerable autonomy, and that rather than giving the audience what it wanted, that is to say being influenced by the cultural or social context, he gave them what he wanted; it was also argued that social and cultural influences are at their strongest only up to the time that a composer puts pen to paper, and that thereafter the music itself suggests its own ideas for development − that is to say that there is an autonomous musical logic. Presumably if this is true for music, it could be true in other creative activities. You have certainly learned that classical and romantic traditions co-existed in the Victorian period: up to a point at least, opting for the classical or the romantic mode may well be a matter of autonomous personal choice rather than something directly socially or culturally constructed.

I hope you managed to put together some thoughts along these lines. In this we have another matter for further discussion and debate in the second part of the course.

6   However writers, composers and artists may operate in practice, it is possible analytically to make a distinction between content (for example, what the painting is of, what the poem is about) and form (what metre the poem is in, whether the movement of the symphony adheres to sonata form, whether the philosophical treatise is in the form of a Socratic dialogue, or a learned article, and so on). But the major point, and I hope you got this, is that the meaning, what is finally conveyed to the reader or viewer, is a result of a combination of content and form.

Perhaps the best way of dealing with this last point is to look at a specific example.

 Exercise

In the *Illustration Booklet*, look at Plate 36, the reproduction of the painting of 1856−8, *Derby Day*, by William Powell Frith. How do you 'read' the painting? In what way does the 'form' contribute to your understanding of the 'meaning' of the picture?

The purpose of this exercise is to focus your attention on the specific connotations of each of these terms, and the interaction of 'form' with 'meaning'. It may help you to know that Frith explicitly stated his objective as recording the detail and variety of contemporary life.

 Specimen answers and discussion

We are looking at a reproduction of a very large painting (note the dimensions 102 × 224 cm) in a landscape format. Nearly half of the upper part of the picture represents sky, and the lower half is crowded with figures. Were we looking at the original, we would have to stand well back to take in the whole. In order to read the details of figure and incident, we would need to come forward, losing sight of the whole, and focus on separate parts of the painting. This reproduces the effect of scanning a panoramic view.

The depiction of distance from foreground to the horizon is, however, subordinated to the representation of foreground incidents, reminiscent of the shallow space and sequential organization of a frieze.

Within this frieze-like composition we can distinguish several focal points, accentuated by effects of light and colour: the countryman in his smock on the extreme left; the acrobats' child looking hungrily at the picnic being laid out by a footman in the centre; the flowergirl offering a posy to the swell, on the extreme right. The actual race course and stand are relegated to the indistinctly painted background. The spectators of the Derby have themselves become a spectacle for the viewer of the painting. Despite the scrupulous attention to details of dress, physiognomy and anecdote, the picture is not a mirror reflection of a real scene. It has been carefully organized to direct our reading of the meaning of *Derby Day*.

The formal elements of the painting: scale, format, composition, light and shade, help us to read the meaning of the picture. Frith presents a great panorama of Victorian society, suggesting the notion of harmony between different social groups, particularly as they are brought together in this great national sporting occasion. A historian could make use of this painting in discussing early Victorian society as a society as much made up of 'estates' as of social classes.

 Exercise

Finally, in this section I want to refer to an issue that has been implicit, rather than explicit, throughout the first part of the course, but which is crucial in our approach to the second part. Consider again quickly extract V.3 in the Course Reader 'Speech by Thomas Babington Macaulay' and extract II.3 'Horace Mann, from the Report on the Religious Census, 1851'. Reflect also on what I have just said about Victorian attitudes to the meaning of 'culture'. Now, very briefly set down the ways in which our attitudes today, looking back critically at Victorian society, differ from the views expressed by Macaulay, the preoccupations of Mann, and the Victorian conception of culture.

 Specimen answer and discussion

We would not today think the highly undemocratic British Constitution as satisfactory as Macaulay obviously thought it, we would not be so preoccupied with religious non-observers as Mann was, and we would, at the very least, be aware of other ways of defining culture, apart from its sense of 'best' artistic and intellectual activities.

Now this takes me to the point I wanted to make. There is at all times a kind of dialectic or interaction between understanding matters as the Victorians understood them (and this is something you must try to do) and at the same time taking the critical position of a student living in the late twentieth century. This is something to be kept very firmly in mind as you work your way though the following units.

4 THE TEN INTERDISCIPLINARY TOPICS

In looking from a historian's point of view at Victorian society I identified six 'essential features'. Some of these undoubtedly contain interdisciplinary elements, for example (3) Town and country and (5) Culture and belief, but fundamentally these were headings which would come naturally to a historian. But in looking at Victorian society in an interdisciplinary way, covering all of the cultural activities (the second definition is implied here), different headings are called for, headings that are essentially interdisciplinary in nature. We have settled for ten interdisciplinary topics which form the basis of the remainder of the course. (The first topic, for reasons to be explained, is in fact quite narrowly historical, rather than fully interdisciplinary.)

Originally, I proposed fifteen interdisciplinary topics to the course team. We felt that fifteen was rather a lot for sixteen weeks of study, and we were, above all, anxious to find important and interesting texts to study in connection with each of the topics we finally agreed upon. 'Nationalism and Imperialism' was among the topics originally proposed, but, since we did not readily light upon suitable texts, this topic was dropped. We do realize that such a topic would have provided material of particular interest to certain of our students. None the less I am certain that you will find the ten topics we finally settled for do provide for a carefully integrated study of Culture and Society in Britain 1850–1890. Here now are the ten topics:

1 Economic, social and technological change
2 Religion: conformity and controversy
3 The impact of science
4 Moral values and the social order
5 Culture: production, consumption and status
6 Working-class culture and the labour movement
7 The role and status of women
8 The representation of the people
9 Town and country
10 Historicism and the concept of 'progress'

Now remember, it is the major aim of the course as a whole:

> to stress the general idea that the Arts disciplines should not be kept in separate compartments, but can and should be brought together both in the study of particular problems and in any comprehensive study of the values and standards of society.

In a way, you could regard our topics as 'particular problems' which, when brought together, do allow for a comprehensive study of Victorian society. The point is that most real problems (and we have certainly listed real problems: 'the impact of science', 'moral values and the social order', 'the role and status of women', 'town and country', and so on) can only be tackled thoroughly if several disciplines are brought to bear on them — if they are tackled, that is to say, in an interdisciplinary way.

Let me now just work through them one by one, bringing out their general significance, and then their significance for Victorian society. Five of the topics actually form the titles for the separate blocks within the second part of the course:

Religion: conformity and controversy (Units 18–19)

Moral values and the social order (Units 20–21)

Culture: production, consumption and status (Units 22–26)

Representation of the people (Units 27–28)

Town and country (Units 29–30)

The topic 'Economic, social and technological change' sets the framework for the whole of the second part of the course, and the other four topics crop up wherever particularly relevant. (The 'Impact of science', for example, is discussed with special thoroughness in the section headed 'Religion: conformity and controversy'.)

4.1 ECONOMIC, SOCIAL AND TECHNOLOGICAL CHANGE

In itself, as noted, this topic is perhaps more basically historical, and less interdisciplinary than the nine other topics. Essentially, a discussion of economic, social and technological change sets the scene for the other topics, but this does not mean that there are not very close interdisciplinary links with aspects of the other topics: for example, social change affects the audiences for particular forms of culture – we may, for instance, in a rather simplistic way, envisage a 'new middle class' with money to spend; technological change affects, for examples, the ways in which works of art can be reproduced; scientific and technological change can themselves be seen as part of cultural change.

In discussing economic, social and technological change I shall in part be building on things you learned in Units 1–3 *Introduction to History*. You must be familiar enough by now with the notion that between 1850 and 1873 Britain enjoyed an unparalleled boom, with rapidly rising wealth, rising profits, and rising prices, and what Best calls 'an economic miracle'; and that, whatever weight we attach to the contemporary label 'the Great Depression', matters were slightly different after 1873. (If you have any doubts refresh your memory by reading the opening pages of Best, pages 19–23.)

 Exercise

Best gives an explanation of rising prices and easy credit. What is that explanation? Do you feel, as I do, that in pages 19–23 Best rather misses the essential factors upon which this 'economic miracle' was based? (If you need a clue, consider carefully the full title of this topic.)

 Specimen answer and discussion

New gold from California and Australia was responsible for rising prices and easy credit. But one would expect Best to say something about technological advance, or rapid industrialization, as the basis for economic expansion.

Technological change

Unit 16 on the Great Exhibition and television programmes 16 and 17 showed how technological change coupled with continuing traditions of skilled craftsmanship were celebrated in 1851 as being at the heart of Britain's industrial prowess and leading international position. At the same time, some contemporaries warned that Britain needed a policy of technological education so that the level of innovation and leadership might be maintained in future.

 Exercise

Try to recall now some of the areas of industry and technology stressed in Unit 16 and television programme 16 *The Great Exhibition I: An Exercise in Industry*.

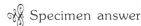 Specimen answer

Some of the ones I spotted were textiles, iron, machinery (including agricultural machinery), steam engines, railways and engineering generally.

With the possible exception of agricultural machinery, Britain was pre-eminent in all of these right up to the 1870s. The mid-Victorian period was one of technological consolidation and industrial expansion, rather than radical innovation. The technology of spinning and weaving that was used in the British cotton industry throughout the century, based on iron machinery and steam power, was established well before mid-century. But after 1850, analogous techniques were developed for the woollen and worsted industries. The technology making possible the production of the vast quantities of wrought iron needed for textile machinery and, especially for railways, was also well developed by 1850. Best's map on page 90 shows just how extensive Britain's railway network was by 1872. We must not forget that the engineering expertise needed for such developments, though based on traditional methods of apprenticeship rather than formal technical education, was considerable and possessed in abundance. Underlying these developments was the exploitation of Britain's vast resources of coal and iron, plus raw materials for the production of essential chemicals. At mid-century, Britain produced over 40 per cent of the world's manufactured goods including half the world's pig-iron; by the mid-1860s it accounted for 60 per cent of the world's coal, and it produced something like 50 per cent of the world's cotton cloth over the period 1850–1870.

Nor should we overlook some of the important service sector technologies. From the early nineteenth century, coal-gas began to illuminate the streets of English towns; by 1859, there were almost a thousand gas works in urban areas throughout the country. One of the great Victorian utilitarian-inspired social reforms was the supplying of pure water and the building of sewerage systems in London and the other large cities. Not only did this involve prodigious engineering feats, it also required considerable administrative expertise. Communications also developed. An electric telegraph system spread throughout the country literally along with the railways, as telegraphy was used initially for railway signalling. Its wider potential for a trading nation with a far-flung empire and military commitments was quickly exploited. By the 1860s, there was an international system of some 150,000 miles; by 1870 England was linked with India and, two years later, with Australia. Aspects of traditional media also changed as steam power was applied to printing presses, photography was developed, and mechanized methods for reproducing paintings and illustrative material emerged.

While the mid-Victorian period was one of technological expansion and consolidation, the late Victorian period, from about 1870 onwards, brought a definite changing of gear. In the first place, instead of being almost alone among industrial nations, Britain was increasingly competing with other industrializing powers, most notably Germany and the USA. There was also a major technological transition, from an economy of iron and steam to one of steel and (at the end of our period) electricity. The distinguished American economic historian, David S. Landes, has written: 'If one were to seek out the primary feature of the technology of the last third of the nineteenth century, it would be the substitution of steel for iron and the concomitant increase in the consumption of metal per head' (*The Unbound Prometheus*, pp. 249–50). Steel, which was a high-quality product combining some of the best properties of cast iron and wrought iron, had long been produced in small quantities for specialist uses. However the invention of the Bessemer converter in the 1850s (stimulated by military rather than commercial considerations), and the alternative Siemens' open-hearth process in the 1860s, made possible the production of steel in the large quantities that began to take place in the 1870s. By the 1880s the output of bulk steel overtook that of wrought iron in the three biggest producing countries, Britain, the USA and Germany.

The availability of bulk steel greatly affected the shipbuilding and engineering industries. In the mid-Victorian period, steam power gradually began to replace sail in shipping and, by the mid-1860s, more iron than wooden ships were being built in Britain. By the 1870s, the greater strength, lighter weight and superior handling properties of bulk steel meant that it was fairly readily substituted for iron in constructing ships themselves and the boilers for marine engines. Special steels also transformed the performance of machine tools which, though considered more characteristic of American industry, were used in Britain increasingly during this period, as were techniques of mass production in some of the new consumer industries manufacturing such products as sewing machines, typewriters and bicycles by the end of the period.

 Exercise

Think back to the questions of historical methodology which you considered in Units 1–3 *Introduction to History*. What are the pitfalls of presenting this sort of hurried overview of technological developments?

 Specimen answer

This sort of overview, largely narrative writing, tends to remove developments from their proper historical context. We must remember that technology too requires analysis as an integral part of the society which fosters it. For example, stressing successful innovations and the magnitude of technological development in our period tends to obscure important continuities. Furthermore, individual technologies should not be analysed in isolation from each other.

For example, one of the origins of railways was local demands for transporting heavy materials in and around coal mines in the late eighteenth century. The development of railways themselves created a greater demand for coal and for other raw materials such as iron, but also made it possible to transport these bulk materials over greater distances to feed other industries. As Best points out, the railway was a major transforming factor in British agriculture as it came to transport foodstuffs over great distances to meet the needs of an expanding urban population. In London, and other cities around the world, rail was crucial for local transport as well. Best's map on page 52 shows the development of a rail network in and around London. The first underground railway, built in London, opened in 1863; it was powered by steam. A horse-drawn tram system appeared from 1870, and the first experimental electric tram car began service in London in 1883. Such developments also had their costs, as Best points out on pages 51–53.

The development of technology is not merely a question of answers being found to problems, nor of bright ideas being pursued by enthusiasts. For example, in the case of the electrical industry, fundamental scientific discoveries making it possible were made by the 1830s. However, it was not until the invention of the light bulb in the 1860s by Swann in Britain and Edison in the USA that there was a mass-marketable product particularly suitable to the new urban societies. Even then, there was another twenty years of commercial and administrative wrangling, competition with gas, and so on, before the first power station in Europe was built in Surrey in 1881. The use of electric motors for industry followed as power suppliers courted wider markets to justify the scale of capital expenditure required for central generation.

 Exercise

Using the index in Best, look up the four references to technology. You will find that he simply has two points to make about technology, one referring to its generally bad effects on the condition of the mass of the people, the other referring to its generally good effects. What are these?

Specimen answer

The bad effect is that of technology throwing people out of work. The good effect is of technology ending the drudgery of child labour.

This emphasizes another point about studying the history of technology. Our own society is only too aware that technology can be a double-sided coin. In studying the Victorian period, we must attempt to understand Victorian attitudes towards technology, some of which were explored in Unit 16. To further your understanding of Victorian views on technology, now read extract I.12 'Second report of the Children's Employment Commission, 1864' in the Course Reader.

Commerce and banking

While industrial developments are of great importance, you should remember that along with them (and not always necessarily directly related to them — for example, overseas trade and insurance were also of great importance) went a great expansion in commerce and banking. Leading figures in these areas were among the richest and most powerful in the land. Well down the social scale there was an expansion in the number of bank tellers, clerks and other white-collar workers. And all of this brings us to the most important aspect of the 'social change' mentioned in the title of this topic: social structure, or 'class'.

Class

 Exercise

I suggested in Units 1–3 *Introduction to History* that there are two main approaches to the study of class. What are these, and what different views of Victorian society do they present?

 Specimen answer and discussion

The Marxist and the pragmatic approaches. The Marxist approach would tend to see a new industrial, capitalist or bourgeois class coming to the fore (sometimes, somewhat puzzlingly, also labelled 'the middle class') and displacing the old aristocratic class. The Marxist view would see this class as being in sharp conflict with the working class. It would usually also recognize that there are other groups in the middle which could be termed 'middle class', if this phrase has not already been pre-empted to describe the industrial bourgeoisie (sometimes there is a bit of confusion with middle class being used both to mean the powerful bourgeoisie, and also the middling middle class).

The pragmatic approach, which is not tied to the notion that a universal 'capitalist mode of production' has replaced 'a feudal mode of production', sees classes not as exclusively determined by relationships to 'the dominant mode of production', but as the products of a number of forces, historical, social and cultural, as well as economic; this approach attempts to understand class as contemporaries in the period being studied understood it, rather than as an abstract tool of historical explanation; it seeks to present a 'map' of the different classes, a picture of, as some sociologists would put it, 'social stratification'. To the pragmatists that phrase is simply an ugly metaphor for what is better described as 'class'. The notion of presenting a 'map' of class structure originates with the early nineteenth-century economist, Patrick Colquhoun, who in 1812 drew up a 'map' of seven classes — the fact that there were so many indicates that the transition from a society in which there are a large number of orders or estates, to a society where there are three or four classes, had still some way to go. Both Best and myself belong to this latter school; Bédarida inclines to the former.

However, for the mid-Victorian period there would be little real difference in the *descriptions* of the class structure given by Marxist or non-Marxist historians (though there might be differences in the *explanations* of how these classes originated, if we were to look into that, which we are not going to).

I hope you were able, at least in broad terms, to express the differences. It is up to you to decide where you stand or, at any rate, to be careful at all times to make sure of the sense in which the term 'class' is being used.

 Exercise

Let us now look at three primary sources in your Course Reader which relate to this vexed question of class: extract I.13 'R. Dudley Baxter, from *National Income*, 1868'; I.19 'T.H.S.Escott, from *England: Her People, Polity and Pursuits*, 1885'; and extract I.20 'William Ewart Gladstone's speech at Liverpool, 28 June 1886'.

1   Read extract I.13 in the Course Reader and answer the following questions:

(a)   Baxter offers a very visual representation of class structure. Make a rough diagram representing Baxter's view of class.

(b)   Why does Baxter prefer the term 'manual labour class' to 'working class'?

(c)   Baxter identifies three classes. He seems to find it difficult to draw a sharp line between two of them, whereas one of the classes he is able to divide off without any difficulty. Which are the two classes he finds difficulty in separating, and which is the class he can separate off without difficulty?

(d)   Basically, how does Baxter define his upper class?

(e)   Do you find that Baxter's account fits in better with a Marxist or a non-Marxist approach?

2   Read carefully extract I.19 in the Course Reader, and then answer this question: How does Escott describe the composition of the upper class as it had emerged in the 1880s?

3   Read extract I.20 in the Course Reader. What is Gladstone saying about the class structure and the relationship of the Liberal Party to it? In what way does the position of the Liberal Party in the 1880s appear to be different from that of the Whig Party in the mid-Victorian period?

 Specimen answers and discussion

1   (a)   Compare your diagram with Figure 1 on page 51.

(b)   Baxter says the phrase 'working classes' is ambiguous and, of course, it is: many people outside the working class do some kind of work.

However, the phrase 'working class' or 'working classes' had become very widely accepted by the Victorian period and it is more sensible to use that phrase rather than Baxter's rather finicky reformulation.

(c)   Clearly Baxter finds difficulty in separating out the upper and middle classes, whereas he has no difficulty in separating off his manual labour class or working class.

(d)   Baxter speaks of those with 'princely incomes', and more specifically of 'great proprietors and capitalists' − he appears to be including both landed aristocrats and capitalists. Note that later he regards *both* the upper and middle classes as having incomes which are 'in great part derived from capital' − so this is not a distinguishing feature of the upper class alone.

(e)   In running the upper and middle class together so that the main divide is with the working class, and in stressing the importance of capital, Baxter is presenting an analysis which could be seen as well in keeping with Marxist theory. But it is not in conflict with the non-Marxist approach either, which brings out that while the two main different approaches have crucial significance in some areas, the differences aren't necessarily terribly important in trying to get a general picture of class in Victorian society.

The best answer would be to say that Baxter's analysis fits both approaches, but if you had opted for either approach giving reasons, you would still deserve great credit.

2   Escott presents a picture of a blending of the wealthy (particularly those with commercial wealth) and the landed aristocracy. He indicates also that it was possible for certain professions to enter into this 'upper class' (note that he does not himself use this phrase), but he stresses that the tone of the upper class is still provided by the aristocracy, 'the aristocratic principle is still paramount'.

For all its gossipy and snobbish characteristics, I think Escott's description, which comes from a general book aiming to identify the characteristics of British society in the 1880s, does give a fair picture of the way in which a new upper class of aristocratic, commercial, industrial and certain professional elements was emerging in the late Victorian period.

3   Gladstone seems to be presenting a two-class picture of society: the classes, the 'very respectable', the 'highly privileged', on one side, the masses on the other. In contrast to Baxter it would appear that he is singling out the upper class, and running the middle class and the working class together. This is scarcely in accordance with the actual realities, but is a rather typical Liberal view of society. In general, Gladstone sees the upper classes as hostile to the Liberal Party, though he recognizes one or two exceptions. This is in sharp contrast with the mid-Victorian period when the greatest and most influential landowners were generally Whigs; now, Gladstone is complaining, most of them and their associated privileged and respectable people (people such as, perhaps, Macaulay had been in the 1850s) do not support the successors of the Whigs, the Liberal Party.

What I would want to add for the *late*-Victorian period (and here there would be a divergence from many Marxist accounts) is that successful members of the former middle class merge into a new consolidated upper class which draws its wealth from many sources and, with regard to individuals, often from several sources simultaneously.

There are then (as we noted in Units 1–3 *Introduction to History*) considerable difficulties in the use of the term 'middle class'. We have to be very careful of the old textbook notion of the early and mid-Victorian periods as a time of triumph for the rising middle class (for example, one could imagine a barrister, or a prosperous Church of England cleric, drawing income simultaneously from ownership of land, investments in both commerce and industry, and professional emoluments). And the landed aristocrats were resilient (remember Television programme 3 *An Historian at Work*).

 Exercise

What does Professor Best say about the position of the middle class in Victorian society? (If necessary, re-read pages 260–8.)

 Specimen answer

Best writes on page 261: 'The middle classes became either deferential or noticeably more deferential than they had recently been. For all their bluster they were, like the archetypal Meagles, toadies at heart . . . From Cobden's point of view, they had sold out to the aristocracy'. The Meagles are the sycophantic middle-class family in Dicken's novel *Little Dorrit* (here middle-class means the middling middle class, and not the ruling class). On page 264 Best quotes an industrialist in the 1860s as saying:

> 'It is not our aim to overthrow the aristocracy: we are ready to leave the government and high offices in their hands. For we believe, we men of the middle class, that the

conduct of national business calls for special men, men born and bred to the work for generations, and who enjoy an independent and commanding situation.'

Thus for the mid-Victorian period we have a picture of a successful middle class happy to go on recognizing the superiority of the old upper class. For the later-Victorian period we have, in my view, not a middle class opposing or overthrowing the upper class, but important elements from the middle class *joining* the upper class so that it becomes more oriented towards commerce and industry than to the ownership of land. Questions arise as to how far it is legitimate to see a middle class which first of all accepts the rule of the aristocracy, and then joins with it, as having distinctively different cultural tastes from the old upper class. Of course, if by 'middle class' we mean essentially those sections that, even after the successful elements have joined the upper class, remain clearly in a middle position in society, then we would almost certainly be right to see this group — which probably formed the main audience for the Victorian novel and for reproductions of Victorian paintings — as having unrefined and slightly 'vulgar' tastes. The best simple question to ask yourself every time you reach for that all-too-tempting label 'middle class' is whether you are envisaging a class genuinely in the middle of society (as the pragmatic historian would do) or whether you are using middle class to mean commercial and industrial interests (i.e. 'the bourgeoisie'), even if you see these interests as occupying a 'top' rather than a 'middle' position in society.

The implication of all this for our interdisciplinary study is that we have to be careful about making rigid distinctions between aristocratic taste and audiences, and middle-class 'bourgeois' taste and audiences. In the mid-Victorian period the middle class tended to ape the aristocracy; in the late-Victorian period we have a uniform upper-class taste to which both aristocratic and former middle-class elements contributed. The important point, however, is that the middle class in the earlier part of the period had a spending power and could create a demand, for which there was no equivalent before the Victorian age, and that the demands of this class and of the subsequent upper class in the late-Victorian period were rather different from those of the more purely aristocratic upper class of the eighteenth and early nineteenth century. There is significant social change and these changes affect what kind of art, literature and music is produced and consumed, but the changes are ones that, in my view, do not lend themselves to any simple formula.

Figure 1   Answer to question 1(a) on page 49

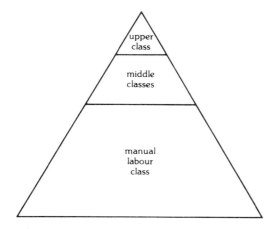

Baxter actually talks romantically of an island consisting largely of a mountain; but what he is really speaking of is a pyramid, which is a manner in which class structure is often envisaged.

Urbanization

As a consequence of industrialization, urbanization had proceeded to the extent, as we already noted, that by 1851 over half of the population lived in towns, and there were already a number of large cities outside London.

Urbanization is a sign of the sort of strength of which the Great Exhibition boasted; but it also brought many problems of public health and sanitation. It is a crucial theme in the study of Victorian society. Page 28 of *Hard Times* gives us a famous, highly-coloured, account of one urban development.

 Exercise

1   Read this account again and decide for yourself how far you feel that it is exaggerated, and how far it gets at the true essentials of urbanization.

2   Turn to Best, and the table on page 29. Apart from populations, we have 'league tables' of the positions of the big towns outside London. Write a paragraph commenting on the changing fortunes of Aberdeen, Belfast, Birmingham, Bradford, Brighton, Bristol, Dublin, Glasgow, Liverpool, Manchester and Nottingham. If possible, try to suggest reasons for their changing (or unchanging) positions.

 Specimen answers

1   This is a brilliant poetic encapsulation, but scarcely an accurate naturalistic account.

2   Aberdeen (a fishing port and commercial and professional centre for the surrounding rural area) is already fairly far down in 1851 after the first phase of industrialization; lacking any major industries it continues to slip down further by 1881. Belfast, particularly important as a centre of shipbuilding, as the 'age of steel' gets under way, moves marginally up the table. Birmingham had been a metal-working centre even before the first expansion of industry in the late eighteenth century; having developed greatly in the first phase of the Industrial Revolution, it too moves up marginally in the 'age of steel'. Bradford, a woollen textile centre, just about holds its own — there is a slippage in 1861, but over the longer period there is no real significant change in the importance of woollen manufactures. Brighton, a most important resort at the time of the Regency (roughly the first two decades of the century), is already well down in 1851 and, lacking any great industries, continues to slide down further. Dublin was still the largest city outside London in 1851, but without industrial development to compensate for the agricultural distress which raged through Ireland, Dublin has slipped down by 1871. Glasgow, still a quiet country village at the beginning of the eighteenth century, was already an important commercial centre (cottons, tobacco) by 1851; with the development of heavy engineering and shipbuilding in the middle and later Victorian period it moves up to the position of being second city after London. Liverpool, though more important than Glasgow at the beginning of the eighteenth century, goes through a somewhat similar evolution but has to give pride of place to Glasgow by 1881. Manchester is often regarded as the classic city of the early Industrial Revolution, centre of the Lancashire cotton industry. With the development also of engineering it moves slightly upwards in the second half of the period. Of all the towns we have looked at Nottingham is the one which shows the most significant upward movement in the league table. With the Nottingham coalfield immediately to hand, it was well placed to develop in the fields of metallurgy and engineering.

Industrialization

In the first version of this unit I did not mention the word 'industrialization', and have been very heavily criticized for this ever since, though actually I do state quite clearly in Unit 1, page 24, that industrialization was 'the single most important force for change in Victorian society', and give a definition. Here is another one: 'Industrialization' means the application of machinery and new sources of power (such as steam) to production, usually involving the development of factories and, ultimately, new mechanized transport systems:

industrialization quickly affects most aspects of life, the development of towns, the further growth of banking and insurance systems, and so on. Industrialization, as the term is usually understood, began in Britain sometime in the eighteenth century. Already by the time the period covered in the second part of our course begins in 1850, Britain was reaping many of the benefits of her early industrialization, as well as suffering from its accompanying evils. During the period we are about to study there came further developments in industrialization, the most important of which have just been summarized for you under the heading 'Technological change'. The reason that I originally avoided stressing the word 'Industrialization' is that I wanted to make it absolutely clear that we were not in this course concerned with the whole process of industrialization, beginning in the eighteenth century and, of course, running on far beyond our terminal date of 1890. I thought that the general topic 'Economic, social and technological change' would adequately describe the extremely important developments which you must understand if you are to understand all the other things happening in Britain 1850–1890. However, if you feel happier in summarizing these major changes under the heading 'Industrialization', as clearly many of my colleagues do, then by all means use that word. Certainly, for instance, all the developments in class which are so important in understanding cultural practices, could be summarized as being the result of the impact of industrialization on a previous mainly agricultural and commercial society. You already know, too, from your reading of Best how important it is to be clear about how far industrialization (which is in turn linked to urbanization, though not all urban development is caused by industrial development) had gone in Britain in the later nineteenth-century (later you will be making a special study of Town and Country). There wouldn't really be anything wrong in speaking of 'the impact of industrialization on later nineteenth-century Britain'; the point I was trying to make in the original version of the unit was simply that it would probably be better and more accurate to speak of 'the impact of continuing and developing industrialization on later nineteenth-century Britain'; just signalling that one is aware that industrialization had begun rather earlier (though its effects, of course, could still be quite new in many parts of the country).

4.2   RELIGION: CONFORMITY AND CONTROVERSY

Religion has been absolutely central in human history and human experience; there can be little point in denying that. The bigger questions of the nature of belief and its social significance call for the skills of the philosopher and the historian: but religious practices and religious institutions also involve art, music and literature.

The Victorian age is often, and not incorrectly, thought of as an age of great religious intensity, of, as the topic title suggests, controversy as well as conformity. There is a sharp contrast with this country today where, by and large, religious feeling plays little part in structuring general political or social thought. Many of the public, political, moral, literary and artistic attitudes of the Victorians were dominated by religious belief. You must at all times try, as I have already stressed, to distinguish between our present-day attitudes towards Victorian religion, and Victorian religion as it was felt and perceived by Victorians themselves.

 Exercise

1   Several times I have stressed the dominant significance of religion. What investigation of 1851, also referred to several times (for example, by Best, by me in Units 1 and 2, in Unit 16, and in *Hard Times*), casts some doubt on the dominating significance of religion for Victorian society?

2   What was Dickens's attitude towards religion?

3   Look at Colour plates 17 and 18 in the *Illustration Booklet*. What do you understand to have been the artist's main religious and/or moral concerns in each?

 Specimen answers

1   The Religious Census of 1851 which in fact brought out how few of the working class were attending church. The point is made by Dickens on page 30 of *Hard Times* when he writes:

> Who belonged to the eighteen denominations? Because, whoever did, the labouring people did not. It was very strange to walk through the streets on a Sunday morning, and note how few of *them* the barbarous jangling of bells that was driving the sick and nervous mad, called away from their own quarter, from their own close rooms, from the corners of their own streets, where they lounged listlessly, gazing at all the church and chapel going, as at a thing with which they had no manner of concern.

2   You may well feel from this, and from Dickens's later joke about the birds being allowed to sing on Sunday, that Dickens was hostile to religion. But perhaps you have noticed a certain religious sentimentality, possibly more strongly marked in other novels, but also apparent in *Hard Times*. Dickens, in fact, like most Victorians of his social position (respectable upper crust of the working class and upwards), was deeply religious; he was, however, as his satirical remarks show, highly critical of the forms of organized religion.

3   For Colour plate 17 *The Light of the World*, it would be difficult to see anything other than deeply emotional and traditional Christian piety; Colour plate 18 *The Awakening Conscience* is more concerned with sexual morality and conscience, but these sentiments are clearly strongly influenced by religious ideas and values as illustrated by the use of a biblical text beneath the painting. Please note that these very bare and preliminary comments of mine will be set in context and developed much more fully in the thorough discussion of these paintings later in the course.

This exercise brings out very clearly the point that to make any comment at all you have first to grasp the basic subject-matter of the paintings. If you were baffled look at them closely again.

 Exercise

I would now like you to consider extract II.3 'Horace Mann, from the Report on the Religious Census, 1851', the document I referred to briefly in the previous section, and which I have already used in Units 1–3 *Introduction to History* to demonstrate the unwitting testimony it offers about the class structure of Victorian society.

1   This extract brings out very clearly a fundamental paradox about Victorian religion: what is that?

2   What main reason is given for the absence of religious practice and belief among the working classes? Do you find this reason convincing?

Write your answers down now, and I will come to mine in a moment. First I just want to make another important point about Victorian religion. Remember the passage from page 30 of *Hard Times* which we have already looked at. Dickens asked: 'Who belonged to the eighteen denominations?' Dickens is referring to the large number of Nonconformist churches which existed in addition to the Anglican church (in Scotland and in Ireland we have very different situations again). The question of Nonconformity is developed fully in Units 18–19.

Specimen answers

1   The paradox is that while the middle classes have become even more religious, and the upper classes have now also recognized the importance of the religious proprieties (thus justifying the view that as far as the influential sections of society are concerned, Victorian society was indeed religious), among the working masses of the population religious decline was serious.

2   Mann's reason is 'unconscious Secularism'. The churches, in fact, offered little which actually appealed to the labouring masses and, despite a large investment of time, energy and resources in seeking to reach them, failed, during the period we are studying, to make any *significant* change in the level of working-class religious observance; beyond that, the labouring masses were fully preoccupied in the struggle for existence (perhaps, of course, that is what 'unconscious Secularism' means).

I do not, however, wish to deny the significance of the movement of secularism. Victorian society became increasingly conscious both of the claims of organized and militant secularism, and also of the depth and seriousness of religious doubt and agnosticism. It is important not to see our chosen period as being governed by one unified attitude on religion (or anything else for that matter).

4.3   THE IMPACT OF SCIENCE

In taking science as a distinct element of Victorian culture, and looking at its 'impact' on Victorian society, we must be careful not to impose views of our own time on the past. For it was a product of the intellectual debates and social changes of this period that science came to be seen as a separate social and intellectual enterprise emerging from a general, unified cultural context.

The amount of scientific knowledge increased strikingly during the nineteenth century. Indeed it was in the 1830s that the word 'scientist' was coined, as a description was needed for the growing number of practitioners in this area of activity. At the same time, the British Association for the Advancement of Science was formed with membership in the thousands; science was enjoying popularity of a highly visible sort. You have seen it parodied, of course, in the opening paragraph of *Hard Times* with its emphasis on facts. However, it is important for us to remember that, for the Victorians, science, philosophy and theology all offered perspectives on the same issues as part of a unified culture which could be (and was) mutually discussed as part of public discourse.

The new scientific knowledge was naturally considered in the debates of the day. With the confidence bred of greater numbers and their new visibility, scientists began to argue a claim for cultural leadership and intellectual priority *within* Victorian culture; the result was the eventual fragmentation of that culture, and a separate role for science. The famous Victorian arguments between some proponents of Darwinian evolution and certain theologians have to be seen in this light, as does the marshalling of 'scientific' evidence and methods in support of competing social and political ideas. These are important issues and clearly several disciplines have to be brought together if we are to grapple with them intelligently.

 Exercise

Look at the opening paragraphs (printed below) of the 'Report of a Committee appointed by the Council of the British Association for the Advancement of Science to consider the best means for promoting Scientific Education in Schools'. It was published in the *Parliamentary Papers* for 1867−8.

1   What does this report indicate about the status of science in Victorian culture?

2   Taking together all of the reasons for studying science given in paragraph 3, try to identify their main emphasis.

1   A demand for the introduction of Science into the modern system of education has increased so steadily during the last few years, and has received the approval of so many men of the highest eminence in every rank and profession, and especially of those who have made the theory and practice of education their study, that it is impossible to doubt the existence of a general, and even a national desire to facilitate the acquisition of some scientific knowledge by boys at our Public and other Schools.

2   We would point out that there is already a general recognition of Science as an element in liberal education. It is encouraged, to a greater or less degree, by the English, Scotch, and Irish Universities, it is recognised as an optional study by the College of Preceptors, it forms one of the subjects in the Local Examinations of Oxford and Cambridge; and it has even been partially introduced into several Public Schools. We have added an appendix containing information on some of these points; but the means at present adopted in our Schools and Universities for making this teaching effective, are, in our opinion, capable of great improvement.

3   That general education in Schools ought to include some training in Science is an opinion that has been strongly urged on the following grounds: As providing the best discipline in observation and collection of facts, in the combination of inductive with deductive reasoning, and in accuracy both of thought and language.

Because it is found in practice to remedy some of the defects of the ordinary school education. Many boys, on whom the ordinary school studies produce very slight effect, are stimulated and improved by instruction in science; and it is found to be a most valuable element in the education of those who show special aptitude for literary culture.

Because the methods and results of Science have so profoundly affected all the philosophical thought of the age, that an educated man is under a very great disadvantage if he is unacquainted with them.

Because a very great intellectual pleasure is derived in after life from even a moderate acquaintance with Science.

On grounds of practical utility as materially affecting the present position and future progress of civilization.

This opinion is fully supported by the popular judgment. All who have much to do with the parents of boys in the upper classes of life are aware that, as a rule, they value education in Science on some or all of the grounds above stated.

✧ Specimen answers

1   Clearly, during the thirty-odd years of the BAAS's existence, the status of science as a subject area had come to be such that considerable pressure began to emerge for it to be included in the general school curricula (for boys). Science had 'profoundly affected all the philosophical thought of the age'. (You would, of course, want independent corroboration of this as a committee appointed by the Council of the BAAS is hardly likely to have argued otherwise.)

2   Apart from the final reason given, the case for studying science in schools rests on its importance as an element of general culture: to train students' ability to reason, to underpin literary culture, to aid in the understanding of contemporary philosophical thought, to give intellectual pleasure.

The final reason is one that we would perhaps most readily recognize nowadays. Indeed, during the period following the Great Exhibition, many were the British proponents of the view that the teaching of science was of direct relevance to future national prosperity. However, at the same time, in line with the justifications for teaching science as a part of general culture, it was also argued that it was important for upper- and middle-class boys to study science so that they would understand in principle what their lesser contemporaries were up to in practice!

4.3   MORAL VALUES AND THE SOCIAL ORDER

Discussion of moral values had traditionally been the province of philosophers. But for moral values we shall have to look also to literature (*Hard Times*, after all, is a moral fable), music and art (remember *The Light of the World* and *The Awakening Conscience*); and for a fully rounded discussion of moral values and the social order we shall need history as well as philosophy.

Domiciled in Victorian Britain were two of the great seminal philosophers of the modern age: the Anglo-Scottish, John Stuart Mill, apostle of liberalism, and the German, Karl Marx, apostle of socialism.

 Exercise

I want you to read the two extracts that follow and state the fundamental difference in outlook lying behind the two extracts.

> . . . there is . . . in the world at large an increasing inclination to stretch unduly the powers of society over the individual, both by the force of opinion and even by that of legislation: and as the tendency of all the changes taking place in the world is to strengthen society, and diminish the power of the individual, this encroachment is not one of the evils which tend spontaneously to disappear, but, on the contrary, to grow more and more formidable. The disposition of mankind, whether as rulers or as fellow citizens, to impose their own opinions and inclinations as a rule of conduct on others, is so energetically supported by some of the best and by some of the worst feelings incident to human nature, that it is hardly ever kept under restraint by anything but want of power; and as the power is not declining, but growing, unless a strong barrier of moral conviction can be raised against the mischief, we must expect, in the present circumstances of the world, to see it increase. (J.S. Mill, *On Liberty*, Chapter 1)

> All previous historical movements were movements of minorities, or in the interest of minorities. The proletarian movement is the self-conscious, independent movement of the immense majority, in the interest of the immense majority. The proletariat, the lowest stratum of our present society, cannot stir, cannot raise itself up, without the whole superincumbent strata of official society being sprung in the air. (Karl Marx, with Friedrich Engels, *Communist Manifesto*, 1840)

 Specimen answer

Mill thinks in terms of the individual, and is already worried by the way in which, as he sees it, society is encroaching upon the power of the individual. Marx writes of social groups: he sees the proletariat as a unity.

4.5   CULTURE: PRODUCTION, CONSUMPTION AND STATUS

With this large and complex topic we come to the very heart of our study of arts and society in Victorian Britain. In the past, if you have studied art, literature or music, you will quite probably have studied them in isolation from the rest of society. You have probably found yourself guided exclusively towards 'great' works of art or literature. However, the whole manner in which literature, music and the visual arts are discussed has changed greatly in the last ten years or so; and in a way that has made interdisciplinary study essential (though, of course, much highly original single-discipline work continues to be done). Academics now ask searching questions about how it is that particular forms of art come to be produced; we are no longer satisfied with the idea of the individual genius doing his or her own thing, irrespective of the demands of the market – we now want to know about the 'consumers' of art, why they provide a market for certain types of art, literature or music, but not for others. As you have already learned earlier in the course, there are many questions to be asked about how it comes about that certain works of art are 'canonized';

we are interested in the status achieved by certain artists and certain works of art; and we are now also interested in popular art as well as 'high' art. Thus, in fact, unlike most Victorians, we will here be using 'culture' in its second sense, to include the widest range of creative products.

Cultural production and cultural consumption

Students (and quite a few tutors!) fret over the idea that art is being treated as in no way different from, say, personal computers, television sets or loaves of bread, which are 'produced' and 'consumed'. ('To consume', I should point out, since some students have been confused, does not just mean 'to eat': when economists talk of 'consumers' they mean anyone going out and buying commodities, whether groceries, or what are often referred to as 'consumer goods', meaning washing machines, television sets, etc.) Now the point of adopting a method of analysis which looks at the way in which cultural artefacts are produced and consumed is not to insist that one cannot distinguish between art and mere consumer commodities, nor that it is impossible to distinguish between 'great art' and 'lesser art' — these are separate issues and a matter for separate arguments: I for one do believe that one can distinguish 'great art' from 'lesser'; some of my colleagues, on the other hand, are very critical of the ways in which some forms of art have come to be 'canonized' — but, as I say, that is a separate issue. The reason for studying cultural production and consumption is that it gives us a very clear and rigorous method of looking at the way in which works of art come into existence: it forces us to look at the very important social context, rather than simply reproducing naive ideas about individual artistic genius. Dickens didn't simply produce his novels in a vacuum: novels were produced in a certain way in his day ('the conditions of cultural production'), first in serial form in magazines (so, just like you producing TMAs, Dickens had to produce each instalment to a deadline, whether 'the spirit of genius' had moved him or not), and then in solid volumes, which would look impressive in the commercial lending libraries (conditions of production are rather different today, when novels are usually considerably shorter than was usual in the nineteenth century — *Hard Times*, of course, is a short novel by Dickens's standards). Dickens's readers, drawn mainly from the middle classes in society, together with the better-off and more respectable working-class elements, had certain assumptions and prejudices: these readers were the 'consumers', and novelists had to pay some heed to their likes and dislikes and their values.

A very important development in the Victorian period is that of the circulation and sale of cheap reproductions of paintings. One crucially important factor in the *conditions of production* here were technical advances in the processes of engraving, without which these reproductions would simply not have been possible. It is the growth of a new market among the lower middle class and upper working class which provides the *conditions of consumption* for these engravings. You can see how the two aspects come together and to some degree determine what art is produced since many artists deliberately began to produce the sorts of painting which could then be converted into reproductions and thus generate a considerable income for themselves and their publishers. Artists, of course, also had to pay attention to the tastes and values of those wealthier people who could actually afford to commission and buy paintings.

So I hope you see there is nothing to be frightened of in these concepts of cultural production and cultural consumption. They form a very straightforward and sensible method of getting at the relationship between cultural products and the society within which they were produced. Of course, the nature of publishing, and the nature of the market for books, do not explain why Dickens continues to be read. The kind of formal analysis you have been taught in the *Introduction to Literature* (Units 4–6) will help you to understand the use of narrative, language, symbolism, and so on in *Hard Times*, all of which have made the novel what it is. You *see* again how the first part of the course is essential to the second part.

Cultural status

The reputation of Dickens has actually had its ups and downs — some Edwardian critics had rather a low opinion of him. Today we tend to think of him as a 'great' novelist: of course, his subject-matter, his preoccupations, were very much those of someone living in Victorian Britain, but he has qualities — such as his humour — which are still recognized in our own age. Reflect for a moment on those two other Victorians Gilbert and Sullivan. Both enjoyed great prestige with the middle class and upper working class in the later Victorian period; now many of us still find Gilbert and Sullivan enjoyable and tuneful, but we would have to accept that Gilbert and Sullivan no longer enjoy even the status they had with the Victorians; their operettas are certainly not thought to be great art. I don't want to exaggerate the change: it would be true to say that among the upper class in the Victorian period Italian and German opera was regarded as 'superior' to Gilbert and Sullivan; and, indeed, Sullivan himself had aspirations towards writing 'grand' opera. But I think you'll perceive the way in which certain works of art can enjoy a high reputation (or status) in one period, and a rather lower one in another.

Richard Middleton has provided me with a fascinating case-in-point relating to the 'First Chord', which you have just been working on. The 'drawing-room ballad' has been mostly the object of ridicule in the twentieth century; and Victorian intellectuals and professional musicians distinguished it from, and regarded it as lower in status than, Italian opera on the one hand, and the 'art song' (deriving from Continental, notably German, origins) on the other (there are some entertaining criticisms of the genre by the Rev. Haweis in the Summer School Texts). Sullivan, and others like him, were looked down on for writing for the market. At the same time, though, for a large swathe of the middle class — the amateur music-makers — the ballad seems to have had quite a high status: certainly in comparison to music-hall song and some earlier forms of bourgeois domestic song (e.g. comic songs from the theatre: glees and catches of, often, a ribald tone). But there were distinctions *within* the genre, mostly to do with the degree of 'formula' or commercial motivation; and there was a historical angle to this: the 'concert ballad' or self-styled 'drawing-room ballad' (like 'The Lost Chord') became separated off from more 'popular' types after about 1870, as the market expanded and its commercial techniques became more blatant and more expert, whereas earlier (certainly in the middle of the century) there was a much easier co-existence of types. Lastly, there were Victorians just as ready as later listeners to treat ballads as objects of ridicule: I'm thinking of the plentiful music-hall parodies of the genre. One might add (finally!) that, as a result of the present nostalgic cult of Victoriana, these songs are now rising in status again, in certain circles.

Given our concern with the relationship between cultural products and society, it is important to know why certain forms of art were valued more highly than others. On the whole (this is a sweeping generalization) most of the Victorian paintings we shall be studying are not terribly highly valued today as art. So when we talk about 'cultural status' all we are talking about is the question of how highly regarded a piece of art was in a particular society. You can learn a lot about the Victorians from studying the kind of art they liked.

Dominant and alternative ideologies

Now that heading is a bit of a mouthful, and we do know that some students blench a little when they come to this as a sub-topic within 'Culture: Production, Consumption and Status'. What you do have to keep reminding yourself, and that is a prime purpose of this unit of course, is that the different parts of this course do fit together and that you shouldn't, once you have finished one block, wipe from your mind all that it has contained. Do you remember when I talked about historical 'hot potatoes' in section 4 of Unit 3? I warned you then that 'ideology' was one of the difficult words that you would have to get to grips with? Let me repeat here what I said on page 96 of Unit 3:

> 'Ideology', in common usage, means 'collection of attitudes and beliefs'. Thus we could speak of Whig ideology and mean 'a general belief in the crucial importance of the landed interest, tempered by a sense that it is the duty of the landed classes to give the country a lead in moving in the direction of moderate reform'; we could speak of John Stuart Mill's ideology and mean 'a commitment to individualism, with a special emphasis on such matters as the rights of women'. We might speak of Labour Party ideology or Conservative Party ideology, though we might have difficulty in putting down anything precise under either heading. We might speak of public school ideology, or feminist ideology, and so on. (Stuart Brown, for the purposes of his analysis in Unit 20, refers to this as a 'loose' definition − 'loose', to my mind, is a rather harsh word for what is, after all, an accepted usage.)
>
> However, in the various forms of Marxist and Marxist-derived discourse, ideology is used in a more specific way, directly related to Marxist theory about class. Each class is seen to have its own ideology, related, though not necessarily in a simple and direct way, to its basic economic interests. In a period in which the capitalist class dominates (many Marxists would see Victorian society in these terms) the dominant ideology is capitalist, or bourgeois ideology. Many phenomena which others might see as on the whole desirable, such as parliamentary institutions or novels with elements of social criticism in them, are seen as essentially products of bourgeois ideology. One might then speak of an 'alternative ideology' of the non-dominant, but perhaps 'rising' class − for example, the working class. (Stuart Brown, in Unit 20, offers a more open version of this definition, defining 'ideology' as 'a set of ideas which serves to foster social cohesion'.)

Now it is in the second, Marxist or Marxist-derived sense, that the phrases 'dominant ideology' and 'alternative ideology' are used in the discussion of 'Culture: Production, Consumption and Status'. It is a purpose of a university course to introduce you to new approaches, to give you the tools with which to carry out serious intellectual analysis, as distinct from simply looking at paintings or reading poems and saying 'I like it' or 'I don't like it'. What we ask you to do is to make the effort to *understand* the mode of analysis which postulates the existence of dominant and alternative ideologies (a mode of analysis which, I have just said, depends also on understanding the Marxist view of class in Victorian Britain). Provided you understand this approach and can *argue* about its validity, you do not have to accept it. In fact, in Geoffrey Best you have already encountered an alternative way of looking at things, a way of looking at things which will be taken up again in the block on 'Moral Values and the Social Order', which you actually come to before 'Culture: Production, Consumption and Status'.

You will get a much fuller explanation of 'dominant ideologies' and 'alternative ideologies' later; here I just offer a very simple sketch. In the Marxist view there is a dominant class in Victorian society, variously described as 'the capitalist class', 'the bourgeoisie', and (very unsatisfactory in my view) 'the middle class'. This class has its own ideology, which, of course, suits its own interests, and particularly its desire to maintain its dominant position and avert protests and revolution from below. According to the Marxist analysis, this class through its dominance over the main means of expression (language, the arts, publishing, the press, entertainments, etc.) manages to persuade other classes (particularly, of course, the working class) to accept this ideology, even though it doesn't really represent their own interests: in this way it becomes a dominant ideology, serving the interests of the dominant class, while keeping the workers quiet by leading them to believe in patriotism, religion, working hard so that they too can get on in the world, the rightness of some form of hierarchy, etc. None of this should be taken as denying that many people within the dominant class who believed in the efficacy of hard work, respectability, self-help and thrift (dominant values), did so, not because these values would help control working men and women, but because they believed they were worthwhile values and fitted into their own moral and religious beliefs.

We do not have to look very far in Victorian society to find that there are people putting forward ideas which do not fit in with this dominant ideology: a good example is the socialist writer, painter, and poet William Morris: thus it is possible to argue that an 'alternative ideology' is being put forward which in traditional Marxist terms, would be seen as the ideology of the working class, the class which is ultimately destined to overthrow the currently dominant class.

You can see that this whole approach depends on a very clear-cut idea about the nature of classes and the way in which they are fundamentally in conflict. Dominant ideology arises 'naturally' from the dominant position of this dominant class, and, whether or not the deliberate policy of members of this class, serves to side-track the aspirations of the working class. The approach is clear, logical and persuasive, and it forms a most effective way of bringing together the texts and evidence you will be studying.

However, if we don't have this particular view of class (the Marxist view) we may prefer an alternative approach. The approach favoured by Geoffrey Best is that of 'consensus'. Best recognizes that there are quite a number of common values circulating in Victorian Britain, such as religious belief, respectability, hard work, thrift, etc. But he does not see these common values as a dominant ideology which the workers are, *as it were*, tricked into accepting: he believes it represents a genuine consensus, a genuine sharing of beliefs amongst all classes. Best, you may remember, doesn't believe that Victorian society breaks down into two main classes which are basically in conflict with each other: he sees society as consisting of a large number of 'estates' linked 'vertically' to each other. However, Units 20–21 will suggest that though Best himself never uses the term 'ideology', it is possible to apply the concept of ideology (in the Marxist-derived sense as expounded by Stuart Brown) to Best's discussion of the 'social order' (an alternative phrase for 'social (or class) structure'). You have just had on pages 48–51, a revision discussion of the pragmatic and Marxist approaches to class. You will have seen how persuasive the Marxist approach is; it has the further great virtue that it meshes perfectly with the approach employing the concepts of dominant and alternative ideologies. Your major task will be to master the concepts of dominant and alternative ideologies. You can then go on and compare that approach with the pragmatic approach or with Best's approach. You may then wish to opt for the notion of consensus; or you might move to some middle position recognizing that there were certain shared moral values throughout all the main classes of Victorian society, but that also there were certain important ideas particular to particular classes, and not shared throughout society (the notion of trade-union solidarity among the working class might be one such idea).

My purpose here is simply to take some of the sting out of these terms. Wait till you come to the fuller discussions till you decide what you are going to make of them. The crucial point is that they are not way-out, or over-intellectual, terms: they're perfectly straightforward once you understand them, and you'll probably find them extremely helpful in your work. Before you can argue on one side or the other (for or against the 'ideologies approach'), you must understand both sides, and really that is nothing like as daunting a task as it may sound at this stage.

Is our course really about Britain 1850–1890?

The biggest single group of complaints we have received about A102 is that the second part, while titled 'Culture and Society in Britain 1850–1890" is really about 'Culture and Society in *England* 1850–1890'. Now here, as it happens, we have a perfect opportunity to apply the dominant ideology approach.

My own personal defence of the course as it stands would be to argue that there was indeed in the period 1850–1890 a genuinely integrated society which can be called 'British society', and that the overwhelming majority of cultural artefacts produced in the period were so similar in form, content, and meaning as to make it perfectly legitimate to speak of a single 'British culture'. On the whole, in choosing our examples for the second part of the course we have tended to go for the more interesting and better known artists. It happens that while Scottish, Welsh, and Northern Irish artists have been prominent in other periods, on the whole their greatest figures were not practising in the period 1850–1890. Obviously, given our chosen dates, we cannot, for instance, put in Burns, Scott, Dylan Thomas or Seamus Heaney (he was, however, along with Yeats, featured in Television programme 5). I do believe that if you, for instance, go to art galleries in, say, Cardiff, or Belfast, or, say, Aberdeen, you will find that local painters of the period 1850–1890 were producing paintings remarkably like those by the mainly English artists we shall be studying. Certainly, two of the better known Scottish artists of the time, William Dyce, and William Bell Scott, seem to have exactly the same artistic preoccupations as certain English artists of the period. Furthermore, whether we talk of shared values, consensus, or dominant ideology, it is clear that some of the key Victorian ideas, notions of thrift, hard work, private enterprise, were most energetically advocated by certain Scots. The supreme popular philosopher of Victorian ideology was without any doubt at all Haddington-born Samuel Smiles, author of such best-selling books as *Thrift* and *Self-Help*. The apostle of work was Ecclesfechen-born Thomas Carlyle. The link figure in utilitarianism between the founder, Jeremy Bentham, and John Stuart Mill, was Mill's Scottish father, James Mill. Gladstone's father came from Leith. Ruskin was yet another England-based Scot.

To repeat, then, my argument would be that, whatever separatist cultures there may also have been, there was one general British culture with highly distinctive characteristics, and to which the non-English contributed. It just happens that the most obvious exponents for us to choose in this course tended to be English.

Now, a strong counter argument to my argument would be that there wasn't truly a common British culture, but that the notion that there was, was *part of the dominant ideology*, neatly suited to maintaining the dominance of the English bourgeoisie. The Scottish figures I mentioned, most of whom settled in England, could then simply be seen as lackeys of the English bourgeoisie. That is an argument you are very welcome to adopt if it appeals to you. But that still justifies us in referring to the second part of the course as 'Culture and Society in *Britain* 1850–1890', the title then being recognized as reflecting the dominant ideology of the time, rather than actual reality.

For myself, to repeat, I don't find that approach necessary: I think a British society and a British culture were realities. How many of you noticed that the cover for the *Introduction to History* (Units 1–3) contained a Scottish scene drawn by a Scottish artist? This Victorian representation of seventeenth-century Riddle's Close seems to me a perfect example of that historicism, that new emphasis on, and new interest in, the past, which is a striking characteristic of *British* culture in the period (part of our tenth inter-disciplinary topic).

Perhaps the most striking omissions, given that we emphasize how important religion was to all aspects of life, 1850–1890, is that of religious developments in Ireland, Wales and Scotland. The simple fact is that, because religion was so important, the slightly different developments in each country are all extremely complicated. We have concentrated exclusively on England, to begin with, because our colleague Gerald Parsons is one of the world's leading authorities on religion in Victorian England. When you see how complex that is, you will understand why we simply did not have space to go into the separate complexities in the other countries. The basic message is that religion mattered very deeply to the Victorians. By all means, if you have the time, read up on your own countries, bearing that message firmly in mind.

4.6   WORKING-CLASS CULTURE AND THE LABOUR MOVEMENT

With the use of the potent word 'culture', this topic both relates back to the central topic I have just been discussing, and also looks forward to slightly different issues: those concerning the nature of inequality and oppression in society, and the manner in which oppressed groups attempt to shape their own destiny.

The British labour movement has many unique features, and it was in the Victorian period that it took on some of its characteristic aspects, and achieved some of its first successes. Thus, in studying this topic, we shall be concerned both with the origins and achievements of the labour movement, and with such questions as: Why has working-class culture assumed the forms it has? How does it compare aesthetically with 'high' culture? What does it tell us about the working class? I need not emphasize that these are interdisciplinary questions.

 Exercise

Turn to the following three extracts in the Course Reader: I.10 'Notes by the Chief Constable of Staffordshire of a meeting of colliers held at Horsley Heath, Staffordshire, 30 August 1858'; I.14 'Letter from S.C. Nicholson and W.H.Wood to Secretaries of Trades' Councils, Federations of Trades and Trade Societies, 16 April 1868'; I.15 'Majority Report of the Royal Commission on Trade Unions, 1867–69'. Read each extract carefully.

1   What characteristic of Victorian society in general, which we have already discussed, comes through very strongly in extract I.10?

2   What do you learn from extract I.10 about miners' wages and conditions?

3   How would you describe the miners' attitudes towards their employers?

4   From all three documents a very clear message comes through about the value of unions and working-class organization. Referring specifically to phrases in the three extracts, say what this message is.

5   What impression do you get of the standard of education of the workers referred to, or involved in, these three extracts?

 Specimen answers

1   The strong sense of religious belief and religious piety. The proceedings begin with a hymn, and the chairman is both a teetotaller and a Sunday-school teacher – though note that we also learn that drinking is widely expected in the coalfields.

2   The wages certainly seem extremely low. On pages 115–17 Best gives some figures for only nine years later when the value of the pound had scarcely really changed, and there he gives a range of from 35 shillings at the top down to 14 shillings at the bottom, with a miner's average of 21–23 shillings. The deductions are noteworthy, particularly the one shilling for drink which would have been supplied to the men while they were actually at work on the theory that hot and arduous physical labour required copious libations of beer (but in practice as a further contribution to the employers' profits). The final sum left for supporting a family seems clearly to be grossly inadequate. Yet even that was not guaranteed with the employers at this stage trying to enforce a further reduction of one shilling. Note that the drinking ethic was so prevalent that the chairman had been turned out of one pit because he would not drink. The highly dangerous conditions of mining are brought out by the

remark of the policeman that they 'would not work in such places for a pound a day'.

3   The key phrase is: 'He did not wish to injure their employers, but it was the duty of their masters to give them a fair day's wages for a fair day's work'. While the workers were prepared to fight excessively bad conditions through strike action, it would appear from this sentence that they did support the general notion of social harmony in relations between different social classes.

4   The message very clearly is that to defend and improve their conditions workers should organize themselves into trade unions (sometimes still called trades associations). Thus, in extract I.10, the brickmaker Job Radford explains how through forming a union the brickmakers now get twice the wages that they used to get. Extract I.14 calls for 'prompt and decisive action' to bring existing unions together in a Trades Union Congress. Finally, in extract I.15 the Royal Commission provides an excellent summary of the advantages to workers of forming unions: they protect them against 'the undue advantage which the command of a large capital is supposed by them to give to the employers of labour'; they seek 'the best rate of wages which they can command, and to reduce the number of hours in which the wages are earned'.

5   The standard of education appears to be high. In the first extract, I.10, we hear that: 'In this great struggle colliers had been working with their brains and had turned poets' − though a few phrases later we do learn of an incorrect spelling. We learn that the first Trades Union Congress 'will assume the character of the Annual Meetings of the Social Science Association', and the papers to be discussed certainly suggest a high level of knowledge. The third extract, I.15, contains less information, but it is noteworthy that substantial, and clearly literate and persuasive evidence, was provided to the Commission by trade-union leaders.

4.7   THE ROLE AND STATUS OF WOMEN

This topic continues the discussion of inequality and oppression in society. It also, of course, links with questions of social morality. One of the great treatises on the subject is John Stuart Mill's *The Subjection of Women*. We shall be examining the role of women in literature, music and art as well as seeking out the historical facts about their earnings, place in society, and attempts to establish early feminist organizations.

   Reflect upon the implications of the painting we looked at earlier. *The Awakening Conscience*; think too about the role of Louisa in *Hard Times* − would it be too strong to describe her as a 'matrimonial pawn'? What is Dickens's attitude?

 Exercise

From this main clause from the Married Women's Property Act of 1870, what would you deduce about the rights of married women *before* 1870?

> The wages and earnings of any married woman acquired or gained by her after the passing of this Act in any employment, occupation, or trade in which she is engaged or which she carries on separately from her husband, and also any money or property so acquired by her through the exercise of any literary, artistic, or scientific skill, and all investments of such wages, earnings, money, or property, shall be deemed and taken to be property held and settled to her separate use, and her receipts alone shall be a good discharge for such wages, earnings, money, and property . . .

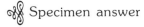 Specimen answer

Clearly women before 1870 were not able to own anything separately from their husbands; whatever they earned immediately became their husband's property.

4.8   THE REPRESENTATION OF THE PEOPLE

My main purpose in introducing the ten topics which make up the second part of the course is to stress how real issues cry out for interdisciplinary approaches. Of course, some issues are more interdisciplinary than others. There can be no doubt about the significance of the topic 'The Representation of the People': the right to vote is a cherished possession, the right to be genuinely represented in government one which is still being struggled for in various parts of the world.

The sequence of events leading to the passing of the Reform Act of 1867 (which, it should be noted, left many people, including all women, without the vote) is largely a matter of political history. But to understand fully the assumptions and debates about the nature of civil society, and about 'representation' and 'democracy', we need to draw upon philosophy.

Two key texts for theories and assumptions about the nature of government are Walter Bagehot's *The English Constitution* (1867) and John Stuart Mill's *Essay on Representative Government* (1861). Bagehot's book was designed to explain how the British constitution worked and, in some measure, to defend it against its critics. Mill's essay is a work of political philosophy which is in part a critique of the existing system of government. For example, Mill thought it was unsatisfactory that the working classes 'may be considered as excluded from all direct participation in the government'. Bagehot, for his part, thought the exclusion of the working classes from 'effectual representation' was entirely defensible. The exercise which follows brings out once again the crucial importance of the careful analysis of texts, before we can go on to develop arguments.

 Exercise

Here are brief passages from these texts in which Bagehot defends the continued exclusion of the working classes from 'effectual representation' and Mill argues that they should be able to make themselves heard in Parliament:

> The working classes contribute almost nothing to our corporate public opinion, and therefore, the fact of their want of influence in Parliament does not impair the co-incidence of Parliament with public opinion. They are left out in the representation, and also in the thing represented. (Bagehot, *The English Constitution*, p.147)

> Does Parliament, or almost any of the members composing it, ever for an instant look at any question with the eyes of a working man? When a subject arises in which the labourers as such have an interest, is it regarded from any point of view but that of the employers of labour? I do not say that the working men's view of these questions is in general nearer to the truth than the other; but it is sometimes quite as near; and in any case it ought to be respectfully listened to, instead of being, as it is, not merely turned away from, but ignored. On the question of strikes, for instance, it is doubtful if there is so much as one of the leading members of either House who is not firmly convinced that the reason of the matter is unqualifiedly on the side of the masters, and that the men's view of it is simply absurd. Those who have studied the question know well how far this is from being the case; and in how different, and how infinitely less superficial a manner the point would have to be argued, if the classes who strike were able to make themselves heard in Parliament. (Mill, *Essay on Representative Government*, p. 225f.)

Note down your answer to this question: Do Mill and Bagehot share the same assumptions as to what political representation is?

Answer

The answer seems to be that they do not. Mill thinks that it is people or groups of people with common interests who should be represented. (He proposed an electoral system which would enable even geographically scattered groups of people to be represented by the same member of Parliament.) Bagehot does not explain 'corporate public opinion', but he seems to assume that a certain amount of education was needed if someone was to 'contribute' to 'corporate public opinion' and so qualify to have his views expressed in the House of Commons.

Mill and Bagehot were not as diametrically opposed as these passages might make it appear. Mill shared some of Bagehot's worries about 'ultra-democratic' proposals, as you will find in Unit 27. The 'one-person, one-vote' view of representative democracy that is now a commonplace was widely viewed by people whose opinions mattered in Victorian society as problematic and even dangerous.

4.9 TOWN AND COUNTRY

Ancient Rome, in its day, was a great city; Roman poets sang of the joys of the country. The theme is a perennial one, and, of course, a marvellous one through which to link novels, poems, drama, paintings, architecture and music. As you have learned from Geoffrey Best, the aristocrats (many of whom, of course, had their origins in commerce and the professions) and the gentry exercised dominance over mid-Victorian society. Many recent commentators (including the American Martin J. Wiener) have pointed out the way in which successful industrialists turned as quickly as possible away from their factories, and the town, and sought solace in trying to live the lives of country gentlemen. A most distinctive feature of the British upper-class family, indeed, was that it divided its time between country mansion and London town house (occupied, in particular, during the London season). The dichotomy, and all the paradoxes inherent in it, is a resonant one. The child of the slums had a stunted life; yet, often, was better off than his poverty-stricken, utterly ignorant, counterpart in the countryside. I make this, not as a categorical statement, but as a preliminary stimulus to the sort of discussion which will arise in later units.

 Exercise

1   How would you describe the relationship between town and country as it is represented in John Ritchie's painting, *Hampstead Heath*, 1859 (Plate 37 in the *Illustration Booklet*)? How typical is it?

2   In what distinctive ways did country differ from town? In what ways, if any, were these differences being diminished towards the end of our period? Base your answer (a few sentences) on Best, pages 84–92.

 Specimen answers

1   Hampstead Heath, to the north of London (St Paul's Cathedral can be discerned in the centre of the horizon) was already becoming suburban, rather than rural in any real sense: as one can see from the painting, various groups of people picnicking and walking have very little privacy from each other. Hampstead Heath, one might say, was a kind of false vision of the country, readily accessible to the teeming population of London. In providing sand for building purposes the Heath actually contributed to London's expansion. In sum the relationship depicted here is of the town (or city) taking over the country. It is not very typical. London as a city was in a class of its own; as you have already learned much of the country was still totally rural.

2   The obvious point (which you quite possibly thought too obvious to note down) is that country is manifestly different from town in being open and undeveloped; on the middle of page 85 Best gives a short description of the countryside as it had been reshaped by the agricultural revolution of the previous century. The country did not change rapidly as did towns, and in particular the social order remained largely unaltered. Roads in the country remained unimproved and inadequate. The main force of change was the railways which, in the latter part of the period, were bringing the countryside into closer relationship with the big towns.

4.10   'HISTORICISM' AND THE CONCEPT OF 'PROGRESS'

Two rather difficult words, and one quite nasty one! Well, if not nasty, 'historicism' is certainly a tricky word, so much so that it is not mentioned in my *Penguin English Dictionary*. In a famous book, *The Poverty of Historicism*, the philosopher Karl Popper gave the word a particular meaning which many people now accept, the meaning of 'grand-scale theorizing about history', as, for example, in the writings of Karl Marx. But this is not the original meaning of the word (though one must accept that it has become recognized usage in certain circles), and certainly not the meaning we intend in this course. Historicism, in its original usage (and in the usage of this course) means a preoccupation with the past, a belief in the essentialty of historical study, a belief that the present can only be understood as an outcome of the past, with the past itself requiring to be understood on its own terms, from the inside as it were, and not simply as a kind of inferior form of the present. In a nutshell: the historicism of the Victorians which you will be studying was a *new emphasis on, and a new interest in, the past*.

৬৪ Exercise

1   The relevance of the Great Exhibition to the concept of progress is obvious enough. But there was also an element of historicism: what was that?

2   Historicism and progress are often presented as opposites but, in fact, they can both be seen to have the same basic attitude lying behind them. Can you explain this?

3   In the discussion of the development of the modern discipline of history in Units 1–3 you encountered a particular academic form of the strength of historicism in the nineteenth century. What was that?

৬৪ Specimen answers and discussion

1   As John Golby explained, there was a certain emphasis on mediaevalism in the Exhibition.

2   Historicism implies a sense of the present developing out of the past. Progress suggests the idea of things getting better and better, from past, from present, to future. In that sense, the two words are simply different ways of expressing the same basic idea.
   However, that explanation is too clever to be accurate for Victorian society. Many turned to the past simply because they valued the past for itself, perhaps like the pre-Raphaelite painters, feeling that art before Raphael was much more honest, much more truthful than, as they saw it, the elaborate stylized art after Raphael. Many questioned the whole idea of progress, the impact of technology, the impact of urbanization, and so on, and also sought a simpler, and as they saw it, better life in the past. Thus, it is perhaps best to see these two concepts as defining two rather different attitudes to be found in Victorian society.

3   The development of professional historical scholarship and teaching

(associated, for example, with the work of Stubbs and with the founding of the *English Historical Review*).

⚮ Exercise

Look at Figure 2. What evidence of historicism can you see in this photograph of Manchester Town Hall?

⚮ Specimen answer

It is built in the Gothic style of the Middle Ages.

Figure 2   Manchester Town Hall. (Photo: A. F. Kersting)

4.11   CONCLUSION

Here, then, are many topics, none of them developed very far, I am afraid. I have tried to reveal the framework upon which the remainder of the course has been fashioned. We want you to understand Victorian society, *both* from the inside (that is, as perceived by the Victorians themselves) *and* as approached critically by us today. But I want you to see that the issues that we are dealing with are, in any context, genuinely important issues. And I want you to see, not just the importance, but the unavoidability of interdisciplinary approaches.

5 INDEXING EXERCISE

At this point we are going to give you some practical guidance for the rest of your work on the second part of the course. What we advise is that, as you complete each week's reading, you should spend some time going back over the material you have just studied noting and underlining any references to the ten topics you have just been reading about and to key people. (By 'key people' I mean those writers, musicians, artists, scientists and politicians who repeatedly re-appear in the course. I shall suggest a few names later to start you off.) You should then transfer those references to a set of index cards (or to loose-leaf sheets of paper), give each card a heading − the topic or the name − and find a place to store them alphabetically.

Before I explain the process in more detail, I should like to say why I think it is important for you to do this kind of exercise. In the first place, the process itself will help you to revise each week's work and to pull together what you have just studied. Secondly, your notes will help you develop a stronger sense of the links between the ten topics and a sharper eye for the extent to which individuals held consistent views, and views which were shared by, or diverged from, those of their contemporaries. Also, your index cards will contain information you can *use*. They should help you with assignment work, when reviewing your study of *Culture and Society in Britain 1850−90* as a whole, and when you prepare for the kinds of essays you will be writing in the examination. Indeed we will refer you to your index cards when we discuss 'Preparing for the examination' in Units 31−32.

Now let us look in more detail at what is involved. Your exercise for *this* week is to look back at Units 16 and 17, and your notes on the television, radio and cassette materials. But before you can get started, you need to make out an index card for each of the ten topics listed on page 44 of this unit. You should do this now. Then make out a card for each of the key names listed below:

Arnold	Eastlake	Mill	Shaw
Bentham	Gladstone	Millais	Smiles
Darwin	Holman Hunt	Morris	Sullivan
Dickens	Madox Brown	Palmerston	Tennyson
George Eliot	Marx	Ruskin	Whistler

(You will not find references to all these people in Units 16 and 17, but you will later on. This list is just to get you started − you will need to add to it.)

The next step is to go back over Unit 16 and mark up references that you think you might want to transfer to your cards (coloured pens are useful for this sort of job). You should underline only those references to people that are relevant to one of the ten topics. For example, you won't necessarily want to note *every* mention of Morris, but only when his views or activities bear on one of these topics. In a moment I shall ask you to transfer your references to the appropriate cards. Before you do so perhaps you'd like to look at examples of references I chose to transfer to just two of my cards — the ones headed *Morris* and *The Role and Status of Women*.

Morris   Cross Ref

1   Unit 16, p. 16: Great Exhibition
    'wonderfully ugly'

    (on Technological Change)   Ruskin (2)

2   TV17 'Approved' Mediaeval Court
    (on Culture)

The Role and Status of Women

1   Unit 16, p. 9: Queen Victoria; example of
    'ideal' wife

2   Unit 16, p. 14: Women's role as domestic
    servants

3   *Hard Times*, pp. 55–7: Mrs Sparsit —   Dickens
    marriage and widowhood

Notice how short my notes are. This is definitely *NOT* the place for detailed comments or for précis; if you attempt to include too much detail you'll soon end up with an unmanageable number of cards. Notice, too, that each entry is a record of the key point being made and precisely where it is made (i.e. it includes unit and page numbers). Alongside such points you should also include references to any material that is used to illustrate them — short quotations (like my 'wonderfully ugly' from Morris), references to works of art and to events, and so on. On 'people' cards each entry will be recording a key point about one of the ten topics, and you should note which topic this is — as I have done, in brackets, on my 'Morris' card. Here I have also included a cross-reference, to Ruskin's view of the Great Exhibition. The number '2' after Ruskin's name tells me that I will find more information about Ruskin's view if I look at the third entry on my 'Ruskin' card. However I have no cross-references, as such, on my topic cards. This is because I need only go to the unit page (or broadcast or cassette) noted by each entry to look for further information. But I *have* reserved a similar space (to the right) of each topic card. I use this space to enter the names of 'key people' beside those points that record their views or activities. (See, for example, Dickens's name beside my third entry on the card headed *The Role and Status of Women*.) The advantage of including such names, in this way, is that it will allow you, later on, to see at a glance the range of key people who feature in discussions of each topic. One word of warning about your re-reading and selection of points to transfer to these cards: I don't think you should always expect the words of each topic to jump out at you from the unit page; some references will be more oblique than others and these you should take care to dig out. (For example, my first entry on the topic *The Role and Status of Women* records a passing comment made about Queen Victoria that is perhaps easily missed.)

I'd like you now to look back at your markings on Unit 16, or to make them now if you have not already done so, check that you want them all and complete the indexing exercise by transferring them onto the appropriate cards. I don't think you should worry about sticking to *my* layout; you may well come up with another which you find clearer and easier to use. I don't think you should worry either if your card entries are not *exactly* the same as mine or those of your colleagues. Indeed, that brings me back to my starting point, for I want you to keep this exercise in perspective. Remember, what we are offering here is some practical advice about *studying*, and studying some sixteen units of interdisciplinary material; so the weekly exercise is intended to help *you*, and is not one you will be assessed on. Essentially, I have suggested a means by which you might usefully review, re-think, and put your own construction upon the remaining course material. I have also advised you to do this work in manageable weekly 'bites'. Left to the end of the year I suspect such work would feel more like sitting down to a rich sixteen-course dinner — rather overwhelming and a sure case for indigestion.

I want to make one final point about this weekly exercise. Your indexing work for the next two weeks will relate to your study of Units 18–19. Unlike Units 16 and 17, Units 18–19 have as their focus one of the ten topics — *Religion: Conformity and Controversy*. Rather obviously, it would be a waste of time and effort to transfer all the detailed points that will arise on this topic to a card with the same heading. Your job in this situation is to look for (underline and transfer) key points which bear upon the remaining nine topics. Although the central topic changes, this point holds good for each of the remaining units until you reach Units 31–32 on revision. There, as I mentioned earlier, we will refer back to all the indexing you have done for the second part of the course.

When you have completed your indexing for this week, and before turning to Units 18–19, you should read your *Library Guide* and listen to cassette 4, side 1, band 1. Both these items will give you further guidance about your work for the second part of the course.

REFERENCES

Bagehot, W. (1867) *The English Constitution*, Oxford University Press (World's Classics edition).

Best, G. (1979) *Mid-Victorian Britain 1851–75*, Fontana.

Golby, J. (ed.) (1986) *Culture and Society in Britain 1850–1890: a source book of contemporary writings*, Oxford University Press (referred to in the text as the Course Reader).

Landes, D. S. (1969) *The Unbound Prometheus: Technological Change and Industrial Development in Western Europe from 1750 to the Present*, Cambridge University Press.

Mill, J. S. (1861) *Essay on Representative Government*, Dent (Everyman edition).

Popper, K. (1977) *The Poverty of Historicism*, Harper and Row.